W9-AKW-365

WITHDRAWN

Marie Curie

GIANTS OF SCIENCE

Leonardo da Vinci

Isaac Newton

Sigmund Freud

Marie Curie

Marie Curie

By Kathleen Krull

Illustrated by Boris Kulikov

Viking

VIKING

Published by Penguin Group

Penguin Young Readers Group, 345 Hudson Street, New York, New York 10014, U.S.A.

Penguin Group (Canada), 90 Eglinton Avenue East, Suite 700, Toronto, Ontario, Canada M4P 2Y3
(a division of Pearson Penguin Canada Inc.)

Penguin Books Ltd, 80 Strand, London WC2R 0RL, England

Penguin Ireland, 25 St Stephen's Green, Dublin 2, Ireland (a division of Penguin Books Ltd)

Penguin Group (Australia), 250 Camberwell Road, Camberwell, Victoria 3124, Australia
(a division of Pearson Australia Group Pty Ltd)

Penguin Books India Pvt Ltd, 11 Community Centre, Panchsheel Park, New Delhi – 110 017, India

Penguin Group (NZ), Cnr Airborne and Rosedale Roads, Albany, Auckland 1310, New Zealand
(a division of Pearson New Zealand Ltd)

Penguin Books (South Africa) (Pty) Ltd, 24 Sturdee Avenue, Rosebank, Johannesburg 2196, South Africa

Penguin Books Ltd, Registered Offices: 80 Strand, London WC2R 0RL, England

First published in 2007 by Viking, a division of Penguin Young Readers Group

1 3 5 7 9 10 8 6 4 2

Text copyright © Kathleen Krull, 2007
Illustrations copyright © Boris Kulikov, 2007
All rights reserved

LIBRARY OF CONGRESS CATALOGING-IN-PUBLICATION DATA
Krull, Kathleen.
Marie Curie / by Kathleen Krull ; illustrations by Boris Kulikov.
p. cm. — (Giants of science)
ISBN 978-0-670-05894-5 (hardcover)
1. Curie, Marie, 1867–1934. 2. Women chemists—Poland—Biography—Juvenile literature.
3. Women chemists—France—Biography—Juvenile literature. 4. Chemists—Poland—Biography—Juvenile
literature. 5. Chemists—France—Biography—Juvenile literature. I. Kulikov, Boris. II. Title.
QD22.C8K75 2008
540.92—dc22
[B] 2007024251

Printed in U.S.A. · Set in KennerlyH · Book design by Jim Hoover

To Caitlin Krull, *future neurosurgeon*
—K.K.

Acknowledgments
For help with research,
the author thanks Dr. Lawrence M. Principe

Special thanks to Janet Pascal, Patricia Daniels,
Robert Burnham and Patricia Laughlin,
Frédérique Moursi, Paul Brewer, Cindy Clevenger
and the Rabbits, and most of all,
Jane O'Connor

CONTENTS

INTRODUCTION   8

CHAPTER ONE
The Gold-Medal Girl   15

CHAPTER TWO
The Pact   26

CHAPTER THREE
Magnetic Attraction   39

CHAPTER FOUR
Mr. and Mrs. Radioactive   48

CHAPTER FIVE
The Legend Begins   59

CHAPTER SIX
Suddenly Famous   74

CHAPTER SEVEN
Shock   84

CHAPTER EIGHT
Embarrassment—on a National Scale   92

CHAPTER NINE
War Heroine   101

CHAPTER TEN
Madame Curie   108

CHAPTER ELEVEN
Genius Genes   115

CHAPTER TWELVE
How She Changed the World   125

BIBLIOGRAPHY   135

INDEX   138

INTRODUCTION

"If I have seen further [than other people]
it is by standing upon the shoulders of giants."

—Isaac Newton, 1675

SHE RISKED HER LIFE for science. That much is undeniable. Yet the myth of the selfless Marie Curie—always with a saintly halo over her head—is far less fascinating than the complex life she did live.

True enough, she was a genius, winning the prestigious Nobel Prize not once but twice, for Physics and then for Chemistry. She married a gifted scientist who dropped his own research to help with hers because it was more groundbreaking work. And she passed on her genius genes to her daughter, who went on to win a Nobel as well.

Marie Curie's permanent claim to fame? She discovered radium and polonium—two new elements, or substances that cannot be broken down any further by chemical means. Lots of elements exist in nature—today we recognize more than one hundred, with new ones still being discovered. But as the Nobel Committee of 1911 pointed out, the discovery of radium in particular was "much greater than the discovery of other elements." The radioactive rays it emits can be deadly, as Marie's own family was to learn, but radium heralded exciting developments for treating cancer and opened a whole new world of atomic physics.

With radium, Marie didn't just make a stunning contribution to medicine. In experimenting with elements that are radioactive—a word she coined herself—she fostered a greater understanding of the very nature of matter. With amazing foresight, in only her second paper on radioactivity, she called it an atomic phenomenon.

The atom: that building block of all matter. Since ancient times, the atom was believed to be unchangeable, indivisible, the absolute smallest thing that exists. But Curie's work paved the way for other scientists to investigate what went on *inside* it. She spurred the discovery of subatomic particles that make up atoms. Ultimately, her work made possible the development of the deadliest weapon in history—the atomic bomb. How she would have hated knowing that! Nevertheless, Marie Curie helped provide the foundation for the atomic age in which all of us live today.

Marie had a tight-lipped, tough side—stubborn, consumed by work, a bit of a martyr. But she wasn't a robot or a goody-goody. Indeed, she said, "I feel everything very violently, with a physical violence."

This was a woman men threatened to fight duels over, someone so passionate about science that she used nine exclamation points to indicate an experiment going well, a person who dreaded publicity and yet was chased by paparazzi. By her mid-thirties, Marie Curie was a celebrity, one of the first people to be the subject of tabloid headlines. Her life story involved broken love affairs, death threats, séances, nail-biting competition, juicy scandal, great losses, and especially a fierce struggle against the strictures of nineteenth-century society. All her life she dealt with "No Girls Allowed" signs—they were everywhere.

Luckily, she had almost limitless reserves of patience. She spent eight years working in unsatisfying jobs before she could get to college. Later, she took almost four years to isolate her new element, radium. What stands out in her story is the amount of persistent hard work that science can entail.

As Marie herself put it: "A great discovery does not issue from a scientist's brain ready-made . . . it is the fruit of an accumulation of preliminary work." Or, in other words, a great scientist is never an overnight success. It takes years of hard work as well as taking advantage of the hard work of other great scientists who came before. As Isaac Newton said in his famous quote, he was able to see further thanks to his debts to others. So who helped Marie to see further?

Robert Boyle, for one, who was an English "natural philosopher" working at the same time as Newton. (The word "scientist" wasn't coined until 1834.) Although he worked as an alchemist, searching for a way to change worthless metals into gold, Boyle also compiled an important book on chemistry. In 1661, in *The Skeptical Chymist*, he laid down some of the preliminaries of this new field, including the definition of an element—any substance that can't be broken down into a simpler substance.

Chemistry took a giant leap forward in the next

century—with Frenchman Antoine-Laurent Lavoisier. In command of the best private laboratory in the world, Lavoisier wrote *Elementary Treatise of Chemistry* in 1789, providing a much more detailed definition of what constitutes an element, and proposing the first table of known elements. Five years later, after the French Revolution, the unfortunate Lavoisier, a well-off tax collector, was sent to the guillotine.

Dmitri Mendeleyev was able to stand on Lavoisier's shoulders even though the Frenchman's head was no longer attached to them. In 1869, this Russian chemist wrote *The Principles of Chemistry*. Inspired by his favorite game—solitaire—Mendeleyev set up a table, or grid, to organize the elements. He used a method similar to the way a solitaire player lays out cards, by suit in horizontal rows, by number in vertical columns. Each row of his table he called a "period." Establishing a pattern, he devised what we call the periodic table of all the known elements. In Mendeleyev's time, some sixty elements were officially recognized—like oxygen, hydrogen, nitrogen, and uranium, discovered in 1798. The table we use today comes from his table.

By Marie's day, the climate for scientists in France had vastly improved since the time of the Revolution.

In part, this was due to the great Louis Pasteur, who in 1868 revolutionized medicine by discovering that bacteria could cause disease. A French national hero, Pasteur inspired Marie by calling labs "sacred places" where "humanity grows, fortifies itself, and becomes better."

In much of her early work, Marie was encouraged and assisted by her husband, Pierre Curie. Work was such a driving force of her life that it's impossible to imagine her marrying anyone other than Pierre, an important scientist in his own right. In 1895, the couple became intrigued with the German Wilhelm Röntgen, who discovered X-rays, and the French scientist Henri Becquerel, who was studying the fascinating rays that were emitted from uranium. Building upon the work of these two physicists, Marie found her life's obsession: adding two new elements to Mendeleyev's table— polonium and radium—and researching them further.

In going on to found the prestigious Radium Institute, she dedicated the rest of her life specifically to providing shoulders for the next generation of scientists to stand on.

In all she did she was brave, undeterred. Both she and Pierre Curie fell sick from overexposure to radium. Yet, as she said in one of her most famous quotes: "Nothing in life is to be feared. It is only to be understood." She viewed science not as a source of pain or martyrdom, but as a heroic adventure: "If I see anything vital around me, it is precisely that spirit of adventure, which seems indestructible." Like a test tube full of the radium she discovered, Marie Curie glows with the pure passion of her commitment.

As for publicity that focused on scientists as human beings, she had this to say: "In science, we must be interested in things, not in persons." So would she have liked this book? Probably not.

CHAPTER ONE

The Gold-Medal Girl

THE SKLODOWSKI CHILDREN were all exceptional. Of the brainy five, the oldest, a talented storyteller, died before she turned fifteen. Two grew up to become doctors. One became a teacher. And the youngest, born November 7, 1867, was to become famous—as Marie Curie.

Education was in Marie's bones. (Her Polish name was Marya and her childhood nickname Manya.) She came from a family of teachers, people who wanted to learn as much as they could in order to change their world for the better, people who believed in great causes. She grew up in Warsaw, Poland, at a time when there was a very real cause to fight for.

Technically, Poland no longer existed. Many people around Marie wore black clothes at all times, in a state of mourning for their former country. Once it had been a mighty kingdom, but by 1795, it had been cut up into pieces claimed by Austria, Prussia, and Russia. Warsaw was under the rule of the Russian czar, who strove to wipe out Polish language and culture. Poles who resisted were sent to the remotest part of Russia—the frozen wasteland of Siberia—and never seen again. Others were hanged—like the brother of one of Marie's friends—their bodies left dangling for weeks as warnings. Many of the most educated Poles chose to leave home rather than risk winding up, in a labor camp or at the end of a noose. Paris, France, became a haven for Polish nationalists working to get their country back.

Marie's father, Wladyslaw Sklodowski, had trained for a career in science, but under Russian rule, Poles were forbidden to work in laboratories. Suspected of being a nationalist, he had to make do with unsteady work as a teacher of mathematics and physics.

Her mother, Bronislawa, was unusually well educated for a woman of her time. After graduating from

Warsaw's best private school for girls, she worked there ever after, eventually becoming the principal. A top-notch education for all five of her children was her highest priority. She even made it known that the better they did at school, the more she loved them.

The family belonged to a part of Polish aristocracy called *szlachta*—they had lost their land and wealth, but not their love of culture. Possessing material goods was not considered as worthwhile as sacrifice in the name of a cause. Bronislawa, with five growing children to support, didn't consider herself above working with her hands. After buying the proper tools, she taught herself how to cobble so she could make her family's shoes. To Marie she was "the soul of the house," a true heroine.

As a baby crawling into her father's study, Marie studied the barometer on the wall, an instrument that recorded air pressure and changes in weather. A few years later, she was fascinated with his locked glass cabinet of physics equipment—shiny glass tubes, scales, an electroscope, which was a device for detecting an electric charge.

Marie was only four the first time she read aloud. Her siblings reacted with shock, which made her

burst into tears—she thought she had done something wrong. By hanging around them, she had taught herself to read. Soon she was helping *them* with their math homework.

Tragedy struck that same year. Bronislawa contracted tuberculosis, a lung disease for which no cure yet existed. The sound of her coughing could be heard all over the house. For fear of passing on the disease, she stopped kissing or cuddling the children. If Marie tried to embrace her, Bronislawa held up a hand to ward her off. She often had to go away for rest cures at sanatoriums in the mountains (fresh air and quiet were believed to help). Zosia, the oldest daughter, accompanied and nursed her mother from the time she was eleven.

When Marie was eight, Zosia was fatally stricken with typhus, another incurable disease. Her death dealt a harsh blow to the whole family, especially Bronislawa, who weakened.

Two years later, Marie wore her dead sister's coat to her mother's funeral.

Afterward she fell into the first of the profound depressions that descended upon her at various points throughout her life. Her way of coping was to shut down emotionally. She hardly spoke and buried herself in books, obsessing about a particular subject.

As times got harder for the family, Wladyslaw temporarily opened a school right in his own house, every corner of it filled with boys, some of whom boarded there. Marie slept in the living room, carving out precious time for homework after others went to bed. Then at six, she was up again to help prepare breakfast for twenty people at a time. Yet her sadness eventually lifted, perhaps as a result of forcing herself to keep so busy.

Education became an obsession. Marie thought of her father as her personal encyclopedia—he always had the answers. All of his lessons had the effect of making her aware of an invisible universe around her. Wladyslaw turned everything, even a walk in the woods, into a moral or educational lesson. Watching a sunset while hiking in the Carpathian Mountains meant a lecture on astronomy. Her father used games and playtime as ways to teach. When the children were young, they spent hours with blocks of various shapes and colors, learning about geography and reenacting battles. When they were older, they clipped pictures from magazines to make collages for their history lessons. Saturday nights they listened to Wladyslaw read aloud, usually novels by the popular English writer Charles Dickens.

He also taught them small ways to resist Russian rule. Above all, it was important to remember you were Polish. Every day on their way to the public school they attended, Marie and her best friend Kazia would spit on a hated Russian monument in the square. In 1881, when the Russian czar was killed by a terrorist bomb, she and Kazia danced with joy in their classroom.

The Polish teachers at school followed a secret curriculum to instill national pride in their students. "Botany class" was really Polish history; "German class" was actually Polish literature. Someone would ring a warning bell when a Russian official approached, so the students could swap their forbidden Polish books for Russian ones. Always the star pupil, Marie was often required to recite in front of officials, the very Russians she despised. Having to play along with the charade, unable to show her true feelings, made her angry enough "to scratch like a cat." But she became good at hiding her emotions when she needed to. Presenting a calm, cool exterior to the outside world was to become a lifelong habit.

At the age of fifteen, Marie was idealistic, with

piercing gray eyes, perfect skin, a mass of uncontrolla-
ble blonde curls. She was shy and insecure, which she
disguised with an attitude of superiority that put off
some people. Although she could speak five languages,
she never mastered the art of small talk.

Upon graduation, she won the coveted gold medal
for best student. She happily presented it to her father,
who expected nothing less. Then she took to her bed,
struck by another depression.

Alarmed, her father sent her to relatives in the
countryside. There she found nourishment in nature—
the mountains, rich farmlands, landscapes dotted with
castles—as well as in the homes filled with books,
music, and art. She had eccentric aunts who smoked
cigarettes and wore pants and ran businesses, uncles
who were talented violinists. One aunt had gone to
a Swiss university; one cousin was a serious student
of chemistry. These months were the only time in her
life Marie had no cares or responsibilities. For once she
relaxed and enjoyed life. She took horse-drawn sleigh
rides with people her age, riding from house to house
to dance the wild mazurka. One night she danced her
red slippers into shreds. She let her brain go on vacation for a year—she rode horses, read "absurd little

novels," drew in her sketchbook. "I can't believe geometry or algebra ever existed," she wrote a bit giddily.

She played practical jokes, though even her pranks
had the precision of science experiments, changing one
variable to test a theory. One relative liked to drink a
whole jug of milk with each meal. Marie decided that
each day she would thin his milk with more and more
water and see if he noticed. Finally he did, to the ac-
companiment of her hysterical giggles. The same relative was the target of a complicated prank, when she
and her cousins turned his too-neat room upside down.
On large nails from the ceiling rafters, they hung his
bed, chair, table, even his shoes, then hid nearby until
he opened the door.

It may seem surprising that a brainiac like Marie
would essentially take off her sixteenth year to fool
around. But she'd reached the end of the educational
road for a girl in Poland at that time. Her brother was
going to attend medical school—and any extra funds
in the family went to support him. Polish universities
were not open to women, no matter how many gold
medals they won. One thing the year off allowed her
was some space to think about life. She didn't want to
be a parasite; she wanted to contribute to society. Yet

how? It was a confusing time. Face-to-face with her very limited options, she still declared, "I, even I, keep a sort of hope that I shall not disappear completely into nothingness."

Returning to Warsaw, she started work as a teacher. At the same time, she continued her studies by taking part in something secret and highly illegal. A group of Polish women were organizing a free academy. Because the women met in different homes, moving from place to place to avoid detection by Russian police, the school was known as the "Flying University." Among the eventual thousand or so women in the Flying University, she met others like her, ambitious and eager for education. She began a program of *self*-education, reading widely—science, politics, literature—as well as illustrating fables, writing poetry, working for an underground science magazine.

In the air was a new fervor for science and industry, previously thought too practical for the literature- and philosophy-loving *szlachta*. Like other young people, Marie admired Auguste Comte, a French philosopher who coined the term "positivism." Positivists believed that scientific and technological advances were the way to improve a society. Intuition and speculation were out. The scientific method was in, using evidence that could be observed, checked, and tested in order to affirm theories. Polish positivism had a special twist— education and hard work would provide the way to rescue Poland. Education, not military might, was the best weapon.

Marie glossed right over Comte's assertion that women were "naturally inferior." Instead, she treasured a contemporary novelist, Eliza Orzeszkowa, who wrote that "a woman possesses the same rights as a man . . . to learning and knowledge."

At seventeen, she still hadn't narrowed her vision to a particular field. Her interests were broad—literature, sociology, and science. Yet already she was entertaining the thought of a career in biology or medicine . . . or perhaps deciphering the mysteries of the elements by using instruments like the ones locked up in her father's glass cabinet.

But how could she go about doing that? Who would help her?

CHAPTER TWO

The Pact

ARIE ARRIVED AT a solution. A far from perfect one, but the best she could devise under the circumstances. She made a deal with her sister, who craved education as much as she did.

At nineteen, Bronia wanted to be a doctor like their older brother. This was an impossible goal for a girl in Poland. So Marie offered to work and turn her wages over to Bronia, so she could go off and study medicine in the intellectual paradise of Paris. In turn, once Bronia was a doctor, she would bring Marie to Paris and help *her* go to college. The sisters placed total trust in each other. Marie put her own hopes on hold.

Being a governess was respectable work. So immediately, she looked around for the highest-paying governess job she could find. She signed on for a three-year position at an estate sixty miles outside of Warsaw: "Scarcely seventeen, I left my father's house to begin an independent life. That going away remains one of the most vivid memories of my youth. My heart was heavy as I climbed into the railway car. It was to carry me for several hours, away from those I loved."

The family who employed her was congenial enough. The father owned a beet-sugar farm and factory. Marie was part servant, part member of the family. She was to teach the family's two girls, one of whom was her own age. Casimir, the oldest son, was away studying math at Warsaw University.

The most meaningful hours in her day were the ones early in the morning before her official duties began and late at night when she had free time. She prepared herself for college, keeping three books going at once on subjects that intrigued her. It was good training, because she became used to working independently. Her father mailed her advanced problems to solve in algebra or trigonometry. She would turn to them, she said, "When I feel myself quite unable to read with profit." And her vision of the future became clearer—what she was most passionate about was science.

A chemist in the beet-sugar factory helped out by giving Marie twenty basic chemistry lessons. She took time to learn all the scientific aspects of farming. She also taught local peasant children how to read and write in Polish—an activity for which, if caught, she would have been exiled to Siberia in the barren eastern reaches of Russia.

Romance "absolutely does not enter into my plans," she wrote. But it did anyway. She fell in love with Casimir when he came home on break from the university. They set about making plans to marry. Suddenly any pretense of treating Marie as an equal was dropped: Casimir's parents didn't want him marrying someone who had to work in other people's houses. Casimir couldn't stand up to his parents. Even more painfully, for several years he kept Marie hanging, on the hope that perhaps they would marry someday.

Staying on as a governess was both a character-strengthening and hideously awkward experience: "In spite of everything I came through it all honestly with my head high." But there was a price. Once again she fell into "deep melancholy." Later Marie wrote a sort of memo to herself: "First principle: never to let one's self be beaten down by persons or by events."

Returning to Warsaw in 1889, she continued working as a governess and kept sending money to Bronia in Paris. But on Sundays and evenings she secretly attended the "Museum of Industry and Agriculture." It was in actuality an illegal lab training Polish scientists, directed by one of her cousins.

At the "Museum," Marie got to work in a real lab for the first time: "I tried out various experiments described in treatises on physics and chemistry, and the results were sometimes unexpected. At times I would be encouraged by a little unhoped-for success, at others I would be in the deepest despair because of accidents and failures resulting from my inexperience." As slow and frustrating as lab work could be, it was also exhilarating, a rush.

Meanwhile, Bronia was reaching her own goal of becoming a doctor. In 1891, she was one of three women in a class of thousands to get her medical degree at the renowned Sorbonne, the central school at the University of Paris. She married another doctor, and with their thriving practice they could finally afford to bring Marie to Paris.

Now, after almost eight years, the escape hatch was lifted. So did Marie rush to buy a ticket and take the next train to France? No. At the last minute, Marie almost gave up her dream, her ambition. Casimir may have still been in the picture. Also her father needed her in Poland. Her vision slid out of focus: "I have lost hope of ever becoming anybody." She was confused, torn: "On the other hand, my heart breaks when I think of ruining my abilities."

Bronia set her younger sister straight. "You must make something of your life," she insisted in a letter, convincing Marie to abide by their pact. Her father, though pained to see her go, didn't hold her back.

In 1891, the twenty-four-year-old mostly self-taught scholar boarded the train to Paris. A thousand miles, three days, sitting all the while on a chair she had brought with her (fourth-class travel didn't provide seats).

Honoring the pact was a turning point in her life.

Paris was . . . amazing, and so different from Poland. There was a glorious sense of freedom. Brand-new contraptions (automobiles) appeared on the streets. Lamps were lit with a new "magic fluid" (electricity). And such beauty—graceful, arching bridges over the Seine River that curled around the breathtaking Cathedral of Notre Dame, monuments like the Panthéon (final resting place for French heroes), lavish theaters like the Opéra, and the newly built marvel called the Eiffel Tower, the tallest structure in the world. Multiple-story apartment buildings with lacy balconies of wrought iron overlooked wide avenues with fabulous bookshops, boutiques and cafés, people strolling about in the most fashionable clothes. Impressionists like Mary Cassatt and Claude Monet wowed the art world. Daily newspapers mushroomed, fueling readers' appetite for any new sensation. Over at the wild Moulin Rouge, the great actress Sarah Bernhardt appeared, as well as other performers, like a man who could fart the French national anthem, and racy can-can dancers memorialized by the artist Henri de Toulouse-Lautrec.

Marie, however, was not a big party girl. She had not come for a good time. She moved in with her sister and brother-in-law in the "Little Poland" area of Paris. It was an hour's commute by horse-drawn bus to her real new home: the Sorbonne. She promptly enrolled in physical sciences, one of 23 women among 1,800 students. On registering for classes, she signed her name as Marie, the name she used ever after. With a bit of struggle, she became perfectly fluent in French (though she never lost her unmistakable Polish accent).

After a few months with her sister and brother-in-law, Marie struck out on her own, determined to take care of herself as cheaply as possible, without any help. She moved to the Latin Quarter, a funky area for students and artists, which was closer to school. She lived alone in a series of unheated attics—what were formerly servants' rooms, often six flights up. In the winter, when the water in her washbasin would freeze solid, she slept with all her clothes piled on top of her. At night, after classes, experiments in the lab, and reading in the library, she ate a piece of chocolate with some bread, or once in a while an egg. One time she fainted on the street. Bronia brought her home and made her stubborn sister eat steak and potatoes.

Yet Marie always recalled this period with fondness, as "one of the best memories of my life." She was happy: "It was like a new world open to me, the world of science which I was at last permitted to know in all liberty."

Even in France, "No Girls Allowed" signs were still around. All the laws favored men—French women couldn't vote, and young girls were educated separately in inferior schools. A popular book of the day discussed the "feeble-mindedness" of women. Female college students were so rare that the word in French (*étudiante*) was also slang for mistress of a male student. "Their study makes them ugly," wrote one wit—they were considered a joke, attempting to change the laws of nature, probably not respectable.

All that mattered to ultra-serious Marie was that the Sorbonne allowed her to keep coming to classes. Her childhood in Poland had taught her how to fly under the radar. She didn't dwell on how unusual she was, never talked about it, and always reported that other students treated her respectfully. Clearly not husband-hunting, she didn't indulge in parties or café life. Now her only social interest was "serious conversations concerning scientific problems."

In these post-Pasteur years, the French govern-

ment was more generous with its financial support
of the sciences. The Sorbonne had new lecture halls
as big as theaters, and shiny, modern labs with state-
of-the-art equipment. Marie's teachers were the best
men in science in France at the time.

Her physics professor, for example, was Gabriel
Lippmann, who invented color photography a few
years later (winning the 1908 Nobel Prize for it). Emile
Duclaux, a cutting-edge researcher and early advocate
of Pasteur's theories, was her biological chemistry
professor. For math, Marie had Henri Poincaré, the
greatest mathematician of his day. Her professors were
impressed by Marie, and several helped her later on at
various points in her career.

One textbook she had already mastered was the
latest edition of Mendeleyev's *Principles of Chemistry*.
His periodic table was a system of ordering the elements according to what a single atom of the element
was believed to weigh (its atomic mass). He went from
the lightest (hydrogen, which became number 1) to the
heaviest.

Among the sixty different elements known at the
time, many had common characteristics in their chemical properties. Mendeleyev saw these subtle, shared

similarities. And when he arranged the elements in horizontal rows of a certain length, he ended up with a chart where the vertical columns were of elements that all shared common characteristics.

He was so sure his pattern was correct that when arranging elements in rows, if the next heaviest known element didn't conform to the pattern, Mendeleyev left a gap in the row and placed that particular element where its characteristics did fit the pattern. He understood that there must be a "missing" element, and at some point in the future, that new element would be discovered and slide into the gap.

In 1875, gallium was discovered, fitting in a gap under aluminum. In 1886, germanium was discovered, fitting in under silicon in a column that also included carbon, silicon, tin, and lead. As other new elements were discovered, Mendeleyev revised his table again and again.

The concept of the atom was nothing new. The Greek philosopher Democritus in the fifth century B.C. had been the first to propose that nothing was smaller than the atom (from *atomos*, meaning "indivisible").

Almost 2,500 years later, at the Sorbonne, the atom was still defined as "the smallest particle of matter."

End of story, no dispute. The nature of the atom was one of the few areas in science that was considered a closed case.

In other areas Marie had professors who said, "Don't trust what people teach you, and above all what *I* teach you." In other words, think independently and test supposed "facts." She was in heaven.

In 1893, she was one of only two women and hundreds of men pursuing a degree in physical sciences. She made herself ill over the upcoming final tests: "The nearer the examinations come the more I am afraid of not being ready." She froze up during the difficult exam and was sure that she'd done badly. But when she went to hear the results of the exam, announced in order of merit, her name was read first. If the Sorbonne gave out gold medals, one would have been hers.

Now what? Something called the Society for the Encouragement of National Industry heard about Marie, this exceptional female student. It hired her to research the magnetic properties of various steels. The project involved work that demanded precision with much testing and graphing.

At the same time, she continued her studies, and in 1894 she earned a second degree, in mathematical sciences. Did she come in first? No, Marie fell all the way to second place. Her plan at this point was to return to Poland and live with her father. With her two degrees she'd surely be in high demand as a teacher, able and willing to help her homeland.

It was in the spring of that year that she met Pierre Curie.

CHAPTER THREE

Magnetic Attraction

SHE HAD HEARD his name before. Pierre Curie was semi-famous. Currently he was head of the lab at the brand-new Paris School of Industrial Physics and Chemistry. It was because Marie needed a bigger lab space of her own that mutual friends thought to introduce them.

Her very first impression was of a "dreamer absorbed in his reflections." Also, "he seemed to me very young." But in fact he was thirty-five, nine years older than Marie.

He was intense, shy, so quiet as a schoolboy that teachers dismissed him, saying he had a "slow mind."

His handwriting was terrible and he couldn't spell. (Today Pierre Curie would likely be diagnosed with a learning disability, perhaps dyslexia.) So he was educated at home by tutors. His father and grandfather, both doctors, taught him how observations could be made about things invisible to the naked eye. At sixteen, he went into physics at the Sorbonne, then into chemistry at the School of Pharmacy, publishing his first article at twenty-one. With his brother Jacques, a professor of chemistry, he was making exciting discoveries about quartz crystals, which would later have applications for cell phones, TV tubes, quartz watches, and microphones. Pierre and Jacques also invented an early version of an electrometer, an instrument that measured electric charges. Other physicists considered it quite cool and were using it.

Brilliant indeed, but Pierre was also known as an eccentric. He was humble to a fault, absentminded. Thanks to his homeschooling, he was not part of the establishment, and he preferred it this way. The school where he worked was not as prestigious as the Sorbonne, but it allowed him to pursue research in whatever he pleased, which was all he wanted of life. His one romance had ended unhappily (when the woman died); he still lived with his parents, under the assumption that a wife would only hinder his work.

"Women of genius are rare," he stated. That was before he met Marie.

"We began a conversation," she wrote later, "which soon became friendly." Friendly talk about science. Pierre was completing his doctorate on the effect of heat on magnetic properties. He was one of the country's experts on the laws of magnetism, and—what a coincidence—that happened to be Marie's area of research as well. Perhaps they spoke about the problem he was currently working on—that at a certain temperature, a substance such as iron or nickel will lose its magnetism. This temperature point is still known as the Curie point in his honor.

His first gift to her was not chocolate or flowers. It was an autographed copy of his latest article, "On Symmetry in Physical Phenomena: Symmetry of an Electric Field and of a Magnetic Field." She was smitten.

He, in turn, was impressed with her independence and her intelligence—she was even better at math than he was. She asked him to her attic room *with no chaperone present*, a shocking invitation. As there was no furniture, she simply pulled out a trunk for him to sit on, and he was charmed.

Idealists both, they wanted to devote their lives to science, though Marie still intended to return to Poland to serve her country. Each so independent, it took some dancing around and negotiating and a few misunderstandings before they realized that what drew them to each other was as important as their commitment to science. In one letter, he wrote that it would be "a fine thing" if they were together, "hypnotized by our dreams: your patriotic dream, our humanitarian dream, and our scientific dream."

How could she resist?

They married in July 1895, in a civil ceremony, with a reception in the garden of his parents' home in the suburb of Sceaux. For wedding presents, they gave each other new modern bicycles, and their honeymoon was spent biking through scenic parts of France.

To begin married life, they settled into a small apartment on the Left Bank, filled with light and overlooking a garden. Their secondhand furniture included a dining-room table that doubled as a desk. Pierre supported them while Marie studied for her teaching certificate, took more physics classes, and did research on magnetism. He had zero problem with her continuing education—they were each other's biggest cheerleaders. He always kept his favorite photo of her, labeled "the good little student," in his vest pocket.

"We dreamed of living in the world quite removed from human beings," he wrote. They spent their evenings reading scientific journals and discussing the articles. He didn't pay attention to what he ate and often couldn't remember whether he *had* eaten. Once in a while they went to the theater or to a brand-new sensation, the movies (pioneered by Frenchmen Auguste and Louis Lumière in 1896). They had little sense of fashion—he wore threadbare jackets and failed to keep his beard and mustache trimmed, while she wore cheap dresses in black or navy blue so as not to show stains from the lab. Their one luxury was fresh flowers in every room.

Four months into their marriage came a remarkable scientific discovery. Not, however, made by either Curie, but by a reclusive German physicist named Wilhelm Röntgen. In November 1895, he accidentally discovered a new kind of ray. These rays had the ability to travel through opaque material that was impenetrable to ordinary light—they could travel through wood, even flesh. The rays were invisible but revealed themselves on a special phosphorescent screen that was standing nearby. Very mysterious. He labeled them X-rays, "X" as in the math term used when a quantity is unknown.

He wrote to a friend that initially he told no one except his wife Bertha about the discovery. He feared people would say, "Röntgen is out of his mind." One of the very first X-ray pictures he made was of Bertha's hand—not only was the wedding ring on her fourth finger visible, but so were her bones. It was to become one of the most famous pictures in the world. Röntgen finally announced his discovery in a dramatic lecture in 1896, capping his performance by x-raying onstage the hand of an eighty-year-old man. Seeing the entire bone structure beneath the skin, the audience rose as one in a standing ovation. Here was a new way of looking *inside* nature, seeing what had never been visible before.

Röntgen refused to patent X-rays for private gain, wanting them to benefit humanity. He later died broke.

Meanwhile, only a few months after Röntgen's X-ray discovery, a French physicist discovered what

appeared to be yet another kind of ray. Henri Becquerel, who came from four generations of illustri-
ous scientists, was studying X-rays and working with
uranium. This element had been discovered in 1789
and named for the then-newest planet, Uranus. Becquerel observed that uranium salts, in spite of being
wrapped in a protective envelope, left a visible image
on a photographic plate. Continuing to experiment,
he discovered something really odd—a constant
stream of rays were emitted from uranium in all di-
rections. It seemed impossible to measure these rays
or to do anything further with them. He assumed
he'd reached a dead end.

Röntgen's X-rays thrilled scientists, especially
medical doctors, who leapt on them with great energy.
Anyone who has ever broken a bone clearly under-
stands their value. One year after the announcement
of his discovery, there were forty-nine books or pam-
phlets published about X-rays, plus over a thousand
papers.

Becquerel's discovery, on the other hand, caused
no such sensation. His rays were mostly ignored. They
seemed much the same as X-rays, only weaker. Just a
day or so after his discovery, he reported on them to

the Monday meeting of the French Academy of Sciences, the most powerful organization for science in France. His colleagues listened, then went to the next item on the agenda. Becquerel himself sort of dropped the ball and drifted for the time being into other areas of research.

Back in the Curie apartment, the nightly discussions were centering on the work of both Röntgen and Becquerel. Marie had published her first article on the magnetism of tempered steels and was casting about for a subject for her doctoral thesis. To earn her doctorate, she had to present original research and make a significant discovery.

Ambitious, enterprising, and always practical, she was attracted to Becquerel's rays by their very neglect. There was so little work on them—only four other papers besides Becquerel's own—she could skip that whole business of reading lengthy lists of background material.

And in her estimation, these "uranium rays" were a new phenomenon that deserved attention. She decided to make a systematic investigation. Uranium had a mysterious way of electrifying the air around it—why? What was the effect of these rays, and where did their energy come from? Were the kinds of rays in uranium to be found in other elements as well?

It was quite stimulating—a new area where she could start experimenting immediately and try to discover something interesting. Even something important.

CHAPTER FOUR

Mr. and Mrs. Radioactive

HE BIRTH OF her daughter Irène in September 1897 barely interrupted the flow of Marie's work. The baby was delivered by Marie's father-in-law, who reported that she never once cried out during the entire labor. It didn't seem to occur to either Marie or Pierre that she might give up research for motherhood. Instead, Pierre's father came to live with them. They also hired a nanny, although according to legend, Marie *never* missed giving the baby her nightly bath. However, little Irène was much closer to her grandfather. He helped enormously with child care as well as housekeeping. When she was old enough to ask why Marie was gone every day while other mothers stayed home, it was her grandfather who explained that Marie was doing important work.

Indeed she was, despite one big problem. Marie had no lab of her own. Pierre solved it by arranging for her to take over a drafty, drab storage space at his school. A closet, really. (On cold days, the room's temperature could drop as low as a frigid forty-four degrees.) Still, it was all hers, a lab she was essentially starting from scratch. Had she worked in a fancy setup within the scientific establishment—say, at the Sorbonne—she might have had to focus on what professors told her to do. Here she was out of the loop, free to explore what she pleased: Becquerel's rays. Passing her during the day, Pierre sometimes would stop to caress her hair.

Pierre was busy with his own work on crystals. Beyond that, his electrometer device was of critical help to her now. With it, Marie could measure very small currents of electricity that the weaker rays of uranium produced.

Pierre also helped Marie construct a chamber out of old wooden grocery crates. Inside they placed two circular metal plates, one at the bottom with a positive charge and another with a negative charge three centimeters above it. A thin layer of uranium was placed on the lower plate.

Marie already knew that the uranium rays would make the air conduct an electric current to the top plate. The more radiation, the stronger the current would be. Using the electrometer to measure the strength of the electric current, she could work out how much radiation was being emitted.

What she discovered was that the amount of uranium was the sole factor determining the amount of radiation emitted (and also the strength of the electric current). Nothing else mattered—not changing the temperature of the uranium, for instance.

The work required incredible dexterity and concentration, painstaking hours of sitting in one position using very precise devices while manipulating a stopwatch and weights. Think of someone juggling while reading a newspaper and you get some idea of the multitasking involved. But this was a job tailor-made for Marie Curie, so careful a worker that at the Sorbonne she was known for never shattering glass tubes the way other students did. She succeeded in obtaining the measurements that gave her the relative power of the uranium.

Now that she'd measured the amount of radiation given off by uranium, the next question was: Did other elements besides uranium emit these strange rays? The only way to find out was to examine all the known elements.

Very persuasive when she needed something for her work, she begged and borrowed samples of elements from other scientists, including some of her old professors. She now went through Mendeleyev's periodic table of elements, testing them one by one. The mystery rays weren't just peculiar to uranium—she discovered that they came in a weaker form from thorium (a mineral element discovered in 1828) as well. Her findings were that only the elements uranium and thorium gave off this radiation.

In April of 1898, Marie made a report to the all-important French Academy of Sciences. The eminent men at the meeting listened to a report on frog larvae. Then Marie's report, called "Rays Emitted by Uranium and Thorium Compounds," was read aloud by one of her professors. She couldn't read it herself because she wasn't a member—no women were allowed. Then came a report on hydraulics. . . .

Marie returned to the lab and kept experimenting.

Now that she had tested all the elements for Becquerel rays, she turned her attention to compound minerals, ones containing some uranium and thorium.

She tested ores just as she had tested each element. Her interest was piqued in particular by a heavy black ore called pitchblende. Pitchblende contains a huge variety of minerals, including uranium and thorium. What she discovered was intriguing: pitchblende gave off four to five times more rays than could have been predicted by the amount of uranium and thorium in it.

Why?

Her leap in thinking was straightforward and brilliant at the same time.

She came up with a hypothesis, a possible explanation that could be tested. A new element, considerably more active than uranium, must be present in the ore. She set out to look for an unknown substance of unusually high activity. "The element is there and I've got to find it," she told Bronia. She was doing something completely new, looking for an unknown element with the only clue to its existence being its strange rays—rays that she called radioactive, meaning active in emitting rays.

To Marie, time was of the essence. "I had a passionate desire to verify this hypothesis as rapidly as possible," she wrote. She was aware of other scientists working in this area already, though perhaps not as precisely and systematically as she was. G. C. Schmidt in Germany, for example, was investigating the activity of thorium. There was a race on—all terribly polite, but still . . . Marie was determined to be first.

At this point, Pierre showed what a generous spirit he had: he could see his wife was on the verge of discovering something major. As brilliant as he was, Marie's work was leading in a more important direction. For a man raised in the nineteenth century, when the second-place status of women—both intellectually and physically—was a given, Pierre did something extraordinary. He stopped his work on crystals and joined her. Marie, who had something of a notebook obsession, had all along been keeping rigorous records of her work. Now her meticulous handwriting was interspersed with his childlike scrawl.

Isolating this theoretical new element involved a process of elimination. All other elements in the pitchblende had to be separated out chemically. After weeks of attacking and reattacking their supply of pitchblende with all the chemicals available to them, the Curies produced something they suspected was their new element.

How could they prove it? Possibly by looking at the light pattern produced by the substance.

During Newton's famous 1666 experiments, he first worked with sunlight and a prism, proving that light contains all the colors. By Marie's time, a whole science—spectroscopy—had developed. In spectroscopy, when an element is heated to a gaseous state and the light it emits is studied through a prism, it produces unique lines along the spectrum of colors. The pattern of spectral lines supplies a sort of signature for that element. Already, eight new elements (including helium) had been identified through their unique spectral lines.

The Curies called in Eugène Demarcay, a French spectroscopy specialist, to help. Alas, no unique spectral lines appeared when their substance was tested. Whatever they had could not be labeled a new element . . . not yet.

As usual, Marie was undeterred. It was her hunch that the substance just needed more purification. After more chemical investigation, on July 13, 1898, she had what she wanted. A new element. She felt secure

enough to give it a name—"polonium," with the abbre-
viation "Po." Pierre wrote it down in their notebook.
Patriotic Pole Marie came up with the name to honor
her native land.

Five days later, at the French Academy, Henri
Becquerel himself read a report by the Curies, called
"On a New Radio-Active Substance Contained
in Pitchblende." (Pierre couldn't read it because he
wasn't a member, either.) It announced the Curies'
discovery of polonium, a substance well over four
hundred times as radioactive as uranium—a new element. It was also the first use of "radioactive" in
print. She wrote that it was "necessary at this point
to find a new term to define this new property of
matter." She had discovered a new element in a completely new way—by its rays.

The scientific establishment understood it was not
dealing with an amateur. Marie was awarded a prize,
money, and a statement that conceded, "The research
of Madame Curie deserves the encouragement of the
Academy."

At long last, the Curies took a three-month
summer vacation to get out of the hot city. Talk
and planning did not cease, especially a hunt for a

supplier of enormous amounts of pitchblende.

Even after the polonium was isolated, pitchblende still gave off an incredible amount of radiation. Did this mean there was yet another new element waiting to be discovered? It certainly seemed that way. After being back at work for six weeks of experiments, the Curies discovered a substance *nine hundred times* as radioactive as pure uranium.

And it produced new and unique spectral lines.

Six days later, on December 20, 1898, she sent off a new paper to the Academy announcing the discovery of another new element. In it she concluded, "The various reasons we have just enumerated lead us to believe that the new radioactive substance contains a new element which we propose to give the name of RADIUM." The name came from "radius," the Latin for *ray*, used for the element's intense radioactivity.

Discovering the two elements had taken one year. Marie couldn't have done it without Pierre's help. They were inseparable. "We really have the same way of seeing everything" was one of his most frequent comments. It wasn't one of those marriages where one spouse's obsessions made the other one feel neglected or envious—they shared exactly the same obsessions to an equal extent. Marie wrote to Bronia (who was in the process of founding a state-of-the-art treatment center for tuberculosis patients back in Poland): Pierre is "the best husband one could dream of. . . . He is a true gift of heaven, and the more we live together the more we love each other."

The lab was a place of beauty, love—and serious accomplishment. By age thirty-one, Marie had discovered two new elements through the rays they emitted and coined the word that described those rays. One way in which she did differ significantly from Pierre was her drive to succeed. He was all but indifferent to competition or taking credit. She was just the opposite—she wanted her gold medals.

Almost from the beginning, she started calling radioactivity an atomic property. She drew the conclusion that the ability to radiate had to be linked to something in the interior of the atom itself.

A year earlier, the English physicist J. J. Thomson, while pursuing Röntgen's research, had concluded that certain rays were made up of particles even smaller than atoms. In other words, no longer was the atom the smallest unit in matter, as Mendeleyev and everyone else had insisted. The atom was *not* the end of the story. Thomson was calling the particles "electrons"—the first *subatomic* particles to be identified.

There was still much more to understand about the atom and its structure. But the doors to modern particle physics—atomic science—had officially swung open.

CHAPTER FIVE

The Legend Begins

*P*OLONIUM AND RADIUM. Both of Marie's monumental discoveries had been based on what she understood to be true from spectroscopic evidence and the intensity of the elements' rays. Now she felt compelled to go further, to produce actual substances that could be seen and measured, so that she could *prove* her theories on a chemical basis as well.

Thus began her legendary quest to isolate the pure radium that existed in such tiny traces in complex ores.

To do so would require huge amounts of pitchblende. She searched far and wide, locating a uranium mine in Bohemia, now part of the Czech Republic. It supplied potters who made yellow glazes from uranium for the vases and dishes that the area was renowned for. The mine was willing to send the Curies ten tons of pitchblende residue, as long as they paid to have it shipped. To the mine it was waste material, basically worthless. All the uranium was gone from it.

To Marie it was priceless. A wealthy baron donated money for the shipping costs. The next problem was storage. Where do you put twenty thousand pounds of pitchblende residue? Pierre got permission to use a huge shed at the school. This was another gloomy place, freezing in winter, boiling in summer, previously a room for dissections, now too shabby and uncomfortable even for that. Foreign scientists who in later years visited the shed assumed it was some sort of practical joke. *This* was where the famous Madame Curie worked?

In the spring of 1899, bag after bag of brown dust mixed with pine needles started arriving at the shed from Bohemia.

Marie's mission was to purify known substances out of the pitchblende residue. First she chemically extracted all the elements that weren't radioactive. Finally she obtained a material that was mostly barium chloride but which also contained radium. At this point she used a delicate process called fractional crys-tallization to separate the barium from the radium. It was a bit like producing rock candy, which is made by repeated heating and cooling a solution of sugar and water. Again and again, she crystallized and recrystal-lized—many thousands of times, all the while striving to avoid contaminating her samples with unwanted substances. It was, typically, painstaking work where she couldn't be too careful. (Later she attributed her success to a very simple rule: "The secret is in not go-ing too fast.")

The shed was filled with vats of liquids she had to move and pour, stirring for hours at a time. It was dirty work, and mind-numbingly tedious: "I would be broken with fatigue at the day's end." She kept track of every detail in notebook after notebook. Accidental contamination and other setbacks occurred often. On the best days, when progress was made, she used as many as nine exclamation points to indicate her gid-diness.

Pierre later said that if the decision had been his, he

wouldn't have persisted with the daunting task of isolating radium, or would have done it later when they
had a decent lab. But like her mother who'd cobbled
shoes, Marie did the hands-on work that needed to be
done, knowing it was for a worthy cause. And always
the drive to succeed—and get credit—fueled Marie.
Pierre was simply not as competitive.

Months passed. Marie worked in her notebooks
at the shed and at home. All scientists are recorders
of events—think of Leonardo da Vinci and his notebooks. Marie was a fanatic recorder. Not just of scientific work. She itemized long lists of expenses ("His"
and "Hers"), wrote down recipes (gooseberry jam, with
ingredients tallied so precisely it might have been a lab
experiment), and especially took note of anything to
do with Irène.

Even as a mother, Marie was a scientist. She noted
daily measurements of her daughter's height, weight,
the diameter of her little head; her first words ("gogli,
gogli, go"); when each tooth came in; every instance
of a skinned knee; all of her accomplishments. In some
ways, Irène was treated like an experiment in progress. And conversely, Marie referred to radium as "my
child."

Through repeated purifications, the radiation kept getting more intense. Something extraordinary was happening. The substance she had isolated *glowed in the dark*. "It was like creating something out of nothing," she said.

After her start in 1899, the months piled up into years. Of their days at the lab, she wrote, "A great tranquility reigned. . . . We lived in a preoccupation as complete as that of a dream." At noon they would break for a simple lunch, perhaps a few bites of sausage with a cup of tea. They had few visitors and participated less than ever in the cultural life of turn-of-the-century Paris.

At night, sometimes the couple would walk the five blocks back to the lab, holding hands, to see in the darkness the eerie blue-green glow of test tubes with radium: "Slightly luminous silhouettes . . . stirred us with new emotion and enchantment . . . like faint fairy light." In their bedroom they kept a vial of radium salts and marveled at its glow before falling asleep.

What the Curies couldn't know, not in 1899, was how extremely dangerous radiation exposure is to all living creatures. Its harmful effects weren't clear for years afterward, and neither of the Curies took precautions while handling it. The excitement of their discoveries was much more on their minds than trivial concerns like a constant burning in their fingers. It was never clear whether the Curies suspected radium's danger; they were part of a tradition of scientists taking personal risks. The oddest example is perhaps the great Isaac Newton, who while studying optics, nearly blinded himself by poking behind his eyeballs with sharp instruments to see what changes in vision the pressure produced.

After reading of two German professors' experiments with the effects of radioactivity on the body, Pierre taped radium salts to his arm for ten hours. A blistering sore developed. It healed slowly, but left a permanent gray scar. The Curies took careful notes, disregarding personal injury, thinking only of the meaning for science. "This shouldn't frighten people," Pierre stressed.

If radium burned healthy skin tissue, could it be used to destroy diseased tissue? Pierre experimented on animals with cancerous tumors—mice, rabbits, and guinea pigs. Yes, he found out, cancer cells could be destroyed with normal tissue growing back. But then, in a later experiment, he put mice and guinea pigs into confined spaces with radium salts. All the animals died in less than nine hours. Breathing radium, it turned out, destroyed the lungs. So how much exposure to radium was too much? That was the ongoing question.

By the end of 1900, the Curies had written six more papers: two by Marie alone, one by Pierre alone, and three jointly. Other young scientists, excited by the discoveries, volunteered to work for them without pay. One was the chemist André-Louis Debierne, one of Pierre's pupils, who continued as Marie's trusty assistant for the next thirty-five years.

In 1900, the Paris Exposition—a gigantic world's fair—drew fifty million people. Surrounding the eleven-year-old Eiffel Tower were pavilions showcasing the latest advances in indoor plumbing, innovations in photography, the brand-new movies, and other wonders of technology. Electric lights were everywhere, and electricity powered a train as well as a moving walkway that took visitors around the whole Expo.

It was an exciting time to be alive. Wireless telegraph service between France and England had just been established, and companies were being formed to sell the relatively new invention of the telephone. People chattered about aeroplanes and horseless carriages. (The Wright Brothers' first successful flight was only three years away, and Henry Ford's Model T only eight years away.) A doctor named Sigmund Freud published *The Interpretation of Dreams*, which would revolutionize thinking about the human brain and further popularize psychotherapy.

The Curies were right in the thick of the excite-ment. As part of the Expo, scientists came in from all over the world for the International Congress of Physics. The biggest draw was the Curies' presenta-tion of their paper, "The New Radioactive Substances and the Rays They Emit." It was their longest report so far, giving full credit to similar work going on in England and Germany. Their conclusion: "Spontaneous radiation is . . . a deeply astonishing subject."

Why?

Because it seemed to violate a fundamental law of nature—that energy could not be created or destroyed. Yet, without diminishing, radium seemed to give off radiation ceaselessly. The Curies made a splash by urg-ing a next step that would solve the mystery. They would locate the source of radiation's strange energy.

Back in the lab, with Marie's legendary labor of love approaching an end, she kept on processing her tons of pitchblende. She found out the hard way that a ton produces only a minuscule amount of radium salt. By 1902 she had a piece the size of a grain of rice. Here it was, physical evidence that proved that radium was a new element. Her discovery was now credible to skeptics.

Marie's work to isolate radium had taken almost four years, during which she lost fifteen pounds and Pierre was constantly ill. Colleagues urged the couple to slow down for the sake of their health. One friend pleaded with them to stop endlessly obsessing about work "every instant of your life, as you are doing. You must allow the body to breathe. . . . *You must not read or talk physics while you are eating.*"

But hard work and sacrifice defined Marie—they were essential parts of her notion of science, and they were essential parts of her very being: "A great discovery does not issue from a scientist's brain readymade." The scientific process was not one of "Eureka" moments but rather a steady, often plodding buildup of knowledge.

At last she was able to calculate the atomic weights of her new elements. Triumphantly she placed radium on Mendeleyev's chart below barium in the column of alkaline earth metals. It belonged in the same column as similar elements, mostly silver-white, shiny metals.

Also triumphantly, she wrote the news to her ailing father back in Poland. While proud of her, he didn't quite grasp the magnitude of her accomplishment, writing back, "What a pity it is that this work has only theoretical interest." He died six days later, incredibly wrong on this particular subject.

Working hard was all the more urgent because the race to learn more about radiation was getting so intense that sometimes mere days separated one person's discovery from another's. This was an epic contest to be first to discover major truths about the nature of our universe. Marie was prepared to do whatever it took to win.

One of her chief competitors examining rays was New Zealand physicist Ernest Rutherford, a protégé of J. J. Thomson, the genius who had identified electrons as the first subatomic particles. In 1899, Rutherford published a paper distinguishing two different kinds of particles emanating from radioactive substances. What he called "beta rays" traveled nearly at the speed of light and were able to penetrate thick barriers. "Alpha rays" were more powerful particles, yet were slower and heavier and could be more easily deflected, even by something as simple as a thick layer of aluminum foil.

Rutherford complained, "I have to publish my present work as rapidly as possible in order to keep in the race" against the "best sprinters," meaning, above all, the Curies.

Meanwhile, the question came up about whether Marie and Pierre would apply for a patent for producing radium. If they kept the secret to themselves, they stood to make a lot of money. No longer on the edge of poverty as they had been during the first five years of their marriage, the Curies were far from rich. All her life Marie saved string, recycled cardboard to write notes on, patched umbrellas to make them last longer, wore dresses until they were threadbare.

But they both vetoed the patent idea. Although aware she was "sacrificing a fortune," Marie believed it "would be contrary to the scientific spirit." Early on she theorized that radium's best use would be medical, and "it seems to me impossible to take advantage of that." Marie and Pierre believed their findings should be available to everyone.

At the same time they were doing their historic

work, the Curies were both teaching in order to bring in money. Pierre began teaching at the Sorbonne. He was a gifted teacher, conveying his enthusiasm and having "the laugh of a child," according to one student. Marie was appointed to the faculty at the premier school for training teachers, in Sèvres, France. The first woman ever. As the lecturer in physics, she was surprisingly awkward at first. Her speaking style was intense, but monotonous.

Curiously, at this point in their lives, they both found time to attend several séances, particularly with a famous Italian "medium." Like some other scientists of the day, the Curies kept an open mind about spiritualism, the belief that communication with the dead was possible. They weren't interested in contacting any dead person in particular, they just wanted to explore the possibilities. "It is human nature to believe that the phenomena we know are the only ones that exist," Marie wrote, "and whenever some chance discovery extends the limits of our knowledge we are filled with amazement." She was talking about radioactivity, but she could almost have been talking about the supernatural: "We cannot become accustomed to the idea that we live in a world that is revealed to us only in a restricted portion of its manifestations."

At séances they took notes, like the good scientists they were. Objects flew around in the air, unseen hands pinched them, and ghosts seemed to appear from nowhere. Pierre, in fact, was starting to spend more time studying the paranormal than anything else. He wondered if it had a relationship to radioactivity—could communication with the dead be another form of energy, one that would possibly reveal radioactivity's source of energy? This line of speculation led to no conclusions.

As a result of her traditional scientific research, Marie Curie received her doctorate in science from the Sorbonne in 1903—the first woman in France to be awarded one in any subject. According to her examination committee, Marie's findings represented the greatest scientific contribution ever made in a doctoral thesis.

At a celebration dinner that night, with several noted scientists attending, Pierre toasted Marie with a glass tube of radium salt in a solution. (He did not drink it, if you're wondering!) Outside in the garden, the tube became luminous, glowing against the darkening sky, illuminating Marie's happy face and also his own burned, permanently scarred fingers.

Theirs was a rare partnership, luminous itself. As Frederick Soddy, another brilliant physicist competing with them, was later to say, "Pierre Curie's greatest discovery was Marie. . . . Her greatest discovery was . . . radioactivity."

CHAPTER SIX

Suddenly Famous

*T*HE YEAR 1903 also brought the Curies the ultimate in gold medals: a Nobel Prize for Physics, shared with Henri Becquerel, for the discovery of radioactivity.

Alfred Nobel, the rich Swedish inventor of dynamite, had established the prizes in 1901 to honor each year's greatest contributions to society in a number of different fields. (Röntgen won the first Nobel in physics.) The Swedish Academy, which administered the prizes, at first was going to exclude Marie. The committee assumed she merely assisted her husband. But Pierre found out and alerted supporters, who successfully lobbied for Marie as co-winner. Even so, at the award ceremony, the committee referred to Marie in condescending terms as Eve, a helpmate created by God for Adam.

To the committee's consternation, neither Curie attended the ceremony in Sweden. These awards were only two years old. Like most people, the Curies didn't seem totally aware of a Nobel's import. Even though a considerable cash award came with the prize, Pierre didn't want to give up the extra money he was making from lectures. Plus he was experiencing pain in his arms and legs, starting to have a hard time getting dressed. Rheumatism, he assumed. And Marie had just suffered a heartbreaking miscarriage.

Before 1903, only the Nobel Prizes for Literature and Peace had garnered much attention in the news. The prizes in science had been considered way too esoteric to engage the general public. Now, for the first time, there was buzz about the Nobel for Physics. A lot of buzz. Marie Curie was an object of intense curiosity. A woman contributing to science? Unheard of. A couple involved romantically *and* professionally? A new concept. Most people didn't know what to make of the Curies.

Marie was cast as the Polish Cinderella, the beautiful poor immigrant rescued by Prince Pierre, toiling on to discover a shiny something that held promise to cure all the ills in the world. Even serious newspapers started articles on her with "Once upon a time . . ." Others turned this Polish immigrant into a French heroine: "Let's not quibble about nationality," wrote one Parisian reporter. Someone in America wanted to name a racehorse after her.

Fame was a jolt. Marie was pursued by an early form of paparazzi eager for any details of her personal life, trying to judge if she was "properly" feminine. Some reporters managed to get into the Curies' house while Marie was out. She would pick up a paper and read descriptions of Irène, of their black-and-white cat Didi, reports of things her daughter talked about.

"We must be interested in things, not in persons," she lectured a nosy reporter. It got to the point that when people approached her, she sometimes denied being Marie Curie: "You must be mistaken," she'd say with dignity, then vanish.

Pierre, who required absolute tranquility around him in order to think, was appalled by the post-Nobel frenzy. He called it "the disaster of our lives." He was in the middle of experiments with radioactivity, pass-ing radium through a magnetic field, and testing the amount of energy it put out by watching it heat water. One gram of radium took only one hour to heat a gram of water from freezing temperature to boiling—an as-tounding source of energy.

Now there were all these distractions from work. He bemoaned "this frittering away of our time."

Their horror of publicity deepened when there was a new baby to protect—Ève, born in 1905 when Irène was seven and Marie thirty-eight. She duly not-ed expenses for celebratory telegrams and a bottle of champagne in her notebook.

Although exasperating for them at times, the Cu-ries' Nobel Prize aroused an abiding public interest in science. The work of researchers was now classified as must-know, their findings fascinating, the people captivating. Science was on the map, an impossible-to-ignore shaper of the twentieth century.

The Curies did appreciate the substantial amount of cash (split 50/50 with Becquerel) that came with the prize. For the first time, they had funds to pay an as-sistant. They also installed a modern bathroom. Sometimes Marie treated herself to a jar of caviar on the way home.

There were professional benefits as well. In 1904, Pierre was appointed to an important professorship in physics at the Sorbonne. The following year, he was elected to the prestigious French Academy of Sciences. This meant access to more funding and power. Electing a woman was, of course, still out of the question. In all of its 238 years, there had been few groups more staunchly male.

Radioactivity was ill-understood by the public, but radium was visible. And highly commercial. Minuscule amounts were put into any number of products. Surely it couldn't be dangerous, when it was touted as the cure for every ill. One ludicrous headline declared, "Radium Makes Blind Girl See."

Quack applications of real as well as fake radium became a multi-million-dollar business. It was put into hair tonic (promising to stop hair loss as well as get rid of gray), toothpaste, lipstick, suppositories. There were glow-in-the-dark costumes for dancers, radiant cocktails at restaurants. Chic people carried tiny vials of radium salt in their pockets, thinking to keep themselves healthy. There wasn't much Marie could do about the bogus attempts to make money off radium, though she did hire a lawyer when an "Alfred Curie" began selling "Crème Tho-Radia."

Meanwhile, real science sped forward. New Zealander Ernest Rutherford, using radioactive materials generously supplied by Marie, was working hard to prove his "transformation theory," which claimed that radioactive elements actually change into other elements. In the process of changing, they give off radiation. He wrote about radioactive elements "which in their disintegration liberate enormous amounts of energy."

In other words, elements like radium were unstable, and in the process of spontaneously breaking down, were decaying into other elements. It was this decay that was sending out energy in the form of his alpha and beta rays.

The Curies resisted Rutherford's theory at first. Could something really be called an element if it was so unstable? But the decay theory had legs. And as evidence mounted, the Curies were gradually coming around to Rutherford's point of view. For one thing, it confirmed Marie's speculation that radioactivity was a subatomic property. There was something going on in the atom itself.

Medicine was the first scientific arena to be affected by radioactivity. In 1904, the first textbook describ-
ing radium treatments for cancer patients appeared.

That same year, Rutherford was exploring what radioactivity might reveal about how old minerals were.
He came up with the term "half-life," which refers to
the amount of time it takes one half of an unstable element to decay or change into either another element or
a different form of itself. Not all elements have a half-
life, only unstable ones. That's because as unstable elements give off radiation, they change.

Depending on the specific material, the half-life
could be as short as a second or as long as a billion
years. But an element's half-life never changed. So, for
example, scientists could figure out the exact age of a
certain piece of uranium by calculating how far it had
decayed. Using this method, Rutherford found out
that a piece of uranium from Connecticut was 550 million years old. Rutherford's work, as he himself said,
"increases the possible limit of the duration of life on
this planet, and allows the time claimed by the geolo-
gist and biologist for the process of evolution." In other words, the aging of elements was helping to prove
Darwin right about the Earth being far older than the
biblical projection of six thousand years.

In 1905, an amateur Swiss physicist, Albert Einstein, also had some thoughts about unstable elements.
According to his calculation (the famous theory of
relativity), very small amounts of matter were capable
of turning into huge amounts of energy. Radioactivity
was an extraordinarily effective means of producing
energy.

In 1906, Marie voiced her acceptance of the decay
theory. Through the decay theory, she was able to re-
fute another scientist's claim to have isolated a new element that was suspiciously similar to her polonium. She
published a study showing how polonium decayed and
became what the other scientist was calling "radiotellu-
rium." But the two had the same half-life and thus were
one and the same. In establishing polonium's half-life,
Marie was shoring up her own discoveries.

Pierre's contributions were diminishing. Dis-
combobulated by the distractions of fame, he wrote,
"There are days when we scarcely have time to
breathe." Still, he noted that Marie "does not lose
a minute" between teaching, child care, and putting
in many more hours than he did at the lab, even finding time for occasional concerts and art exhibits. Of
course, Marie as usual pushed herself to the point of
overload. One of Ève's very first memories was of her

exhausted mother fainting and falling to the floor.

In 1904, Marie wrote a magazine article detailing her discoveries so far, ending with a very practical plea for more resources to continue their work: "At the present time we possess only about a gram of pure salts of radium. Research in all branches of experimental science—physics, chemistry, physiology, medicine—is impeded, and a whole evolution in science is retarded, by the lack of this precious and unique material, which can now be obtained only at great expense." Years would pass before her plea was answered, but in the meantime she was always generous in supplying fellow researchers with samples of what she produced, allow-ing competitors to make further discoveries. Marie even gave free consultation to factories in the United States, who adopted her method for extracting radium to produce commercial products.

Finally finding a moment to take a break, the Cu-ries traveled in 1905 to Sweden to give their Nobel lec-ture at the Swedish Academy. Pierre was designated to give the speech (Marie had to sit in the audience!), but her husband gave her full credit, mentioning her name ten times and himself only five.

His speech has become famous for its dark predic-tion. For the first time, someone was prophesying the potential for evil from radium, which unleashed such tremendous energy: "Radium could become very dangerous in criminal hands," warned Pierre—"a terrible means of destruction in the hands of criminals who are leading the people toward war."

Still, he remained firmly in the camp of those convinced that radium would do more good than harm, and that discovering the secrets of nature was worth the risk.

But by this time, his leg bones were deteriorating. Some days he could barely stand upright. He was forty-eight years old. Not young. But not old.

CHAPTER SEVEN

Shock

"WE WERE HAPPY," Marie wrote about the family's Easter vacation in April 1906. Everyone frolicked in the countryside, enjoying the signs of spring, both parents watching their girls chasing butterflies, Pierre picking bouquets of marigolds for Marie.

But she was not pleased when he returned to Paris early to do some work. Nor did her mood improve when she and the children arrived home. In a rare instance of role reversal, she and Pierre argued because he was anxious for her to join him in the lab right away. Marie, normally the obsessive workaholic, wanted her break to last a little longer.

"Don't torment me," she told her husband on his way out the door—a clue that her life was more a precarious balancing act than she publicly let on. On this crucial day, she chose to be with her children instead of in the lab.

The day was chilly and rainy. Pierre went from the lab to a business lunch, then later walked to the library from the Sorbonne. Stepping off a curb into the most crowded intersection in Paris, he walked straight into the path of a horse-drawn wagon. It dragged him under, crushing his skull.

He died instantly.

Would he have been able to avoid the fall if his legs had been stronger? Was he daydreaming, instead of paying attention to the traffic? Or was he thinking about his last unpleasant conversation with Marie? What if the day hadn't been rainy and an umbrella hadn't obscured his vision? Of all the questions, the one that most taunted Marie was why had her last words to him been reproachful, so harsh and uncharacteristic of their love?

The sudden death of her husband at age forty-nine was a horrific blow, the loss of her best friend, soul mate, the source of her serenity, the devoted father of her two daughters, and her only real peer in science.

She described her feeling as "wanting to scream like a savage beast."

But she didn't scream. Not out loud. Nor did she talk about him; around the children she never allowed his name to be spoken. In a way today's child psychologists wouldn't applaud, she assumed that erasing Pierre would enable baby Ève and nine-year-old Irène to get over their father's death more quickly. We don't know whether Marie ever read Freud and his theories about the negative consequences of repressing feelings, but from her actions it seems unlikely. Not only was Pierre gone, she now became her most remote as a mother, leaving it to the children's grandfather to provide emotional comfort. She did start a new notebook, of tan canvas, a journal addressing Pierre as if he were still alive, hoping against hope that communication was still possible: "I live only for your memory and to make you proud of me." She was comforted that maybe "an accumulation of energy" had come from his casket toward her during the funeral.

Although there were moments when she forgot the pain, for a long time afterward she would be overtaken by "the feeling of obsessive distress." As always, she dealt with a black depression by escaping into work. Three days after the accident, she was back in the lab, starting another new notebook of experiments, refining work of Pierre's. "I no longer know what joy is or even pleasure," she wrote in her mourning notebook. "I will never be able to laugh genuinely until the end of my days."

When the French government offered her a pension, she refused it, basically saying, "I am thirty-nine and able to support myself, thank you very much." No longer part of a team, she was still a scientist in her own right. An increasingly respected one. It was a turning point, going from a duo to a solo.

She devoted all her energy to continuing alone the work they had undertaken together. In her mourning notebook she confessed her motivation came from "the desire to prove to the world, and above all to myself, that that which you loved so much has some real value."

She proved it in grand style in 1909, when the University of Paris and the Pasteur Institute decided to join forces to build her a large laboratory from scratch. She had always loved Louis Pasteur's reference to labs as "sacred places" where "humanity grows, fortifies itself, and becomes better." Now she would have a sacred place of her own. Marie involved herself in every detail of her new Radium Institute, to be erected a few streets away from the now-famous "shed."

She was also hard at work on her exhaustive summary of radioactivity, which was eventually published in 1910. The two-volume *Treatise on Radioactivity* provided others with a clear, useful history. That same year, she finally succeeded in isolating radium in its purest form yet.

She kept up with the ongoing research of others. Unlike Mendeleyev, she changed with the times. The temperamental Russian chemist had kept on revising his table of elements until his death in 1907, but he'd fallen out of the mainstream, refusing to recognize the existence of radioactivity or the electron or other new discoveries.

Marie was impressed with the young Albert Einstein and wrote him a letter of recommendation for a position at the University of Zurich. He in turn admired her "sparkling intelligence," though once complained in private that she was "cold as a herring."

In 1911, Rutherford made another breakthrough, building upon J. J. Thomson's earlier theory about the structure of the atom. In an experiment, a sheet of thin gold foil was bombarded with high-velocity alpha-ray particles. As expected, most passed through and came out the other side. But some bounced back. When Rutherford learned of this, he rightly leaped to the notion that there was a dense core at the center of the gold atoms that had deflected the rays. He labeled this dense core the "nucleus." He outlined a new model for the atom: mostly empty space, with a hard nucleus inside.

Marie paid close attention. After all, it was her isolation of radium that provided the key to the new field of radioactivity. She had created what she later called "a chemistry of the invisible." It was now the age of nuclear physics, concerned with the nucleus of the atom, or subatomic particles.

At the same time Marie was keeping au courant in atomic physics, she had two young girls to raise. Because of her disdain for French schools, she threw her energy into organizing an experimental school for ten children—Irène as well as the children of Sorbonne professors who agreed to teach there. The experimental school lasted for two years, a chance for lucky children to learn from top-notch scholars. She herself taught physics and the first course ever on radioactivity. Like her father, Marie believed that science should be taught early but not too rigidly, with lots of hands-on experiments as well as time for games and physical activities. Her students, for example, proved that heavier bodies fall at the same rate as lighter ones by dipping bicycle ball bearings in ink and then watching the ink trails left as the ball bearings fell down slanted surfaces.

Sadly she admitted, "I want to bring up my children as well as possible, but even they cannot awaken life in me." Her emotions frozen, she was more dutiful than loving. It was most crucial to her that the girls become "invulnerable." At home she made sure her daughters exercised every day, installing a trapeze and other gym equipment in the backyard, making time for bike trips, swimming lessons, tennis games, horseback riding. Pierre's father, still the perfect babysitter, kept the household running, with help from maids and occasionally cooks.

As the only one qualified to take Pierre's place, Marie also became the first woman lecturer at the Sorbonne. She was appointed to take over his classes, but not—horrors—to receive a full professorship with all its benefits. (That didn't come until two years later.) On the day of her first lecture, hundreds came, including Irène, photographers, socialites in enormous hats, gawkers perhaps expecting an emotional outburst.

Instead, tense and pale, she started out: "When we examine our recent progress in the domain of physics, a period of time that comprises only a dozen years, we are certainly struck by an evolution that has nourished fundamental notions regarding the nature of electricity and of matter."

Not many of the casual spectators realized it, but those had been the exact final words of Pierre's last lecture, and she went on from there, seamlessly integrating her words with his.

CHAPTER EIGHT

Embarrassment—on a National Scale

ONE NIGHT IN 1910, Marie arrived at a dinner wearing a white dress with a pink rose pinned to it, instead of her plain black mourning attire. What sort of announcement was she making? Whom was she hoping to impress?

As solitary as she sometimes seemed, she did have a small circle of loyal friends. One was physicist Paul Langevin, a former star student of Pierre's. Einstein once said that if he hadn't already come up with the special theory of relativity, Langevin would have. Marie admired his "wonderful intelligence" . . . and perhaps also his stylish handlebar mustache. He was five years her junior and currently working with electron theory and magnetism.

He was also a married man with four children, though his marriage had long been an unhappy one. He and Marie fell in love, attended conferences to-gether, and eventually rented a small apartment near the Sorbonne as a secret meeting place. She would leave the lab at noon, go grocery-shopping, have lunch with him at the apartment. They exchanged mushy letters: "I am so impatient to see you" . . . "I embrace you with all my tenderness." In one she offered a list of suggestions for extricating himself from his marriage, so precise they read like a science experiment. To her, Langevin was a second chance at happiness with a pro-tégé of Pierre's, a scientific peer; she even envisioned having more children.

Emboldened on all fronts, she allowed colleagues to nominate her for membership in the all-male Academy of Sciences, the most powerful science organization in France. After all, she was already a member of equiva-lent academies in Poland, Holland, Sweden, the United States, and Russia. Still, "science is useless to women," raved a French woman writer in one newspaper. Marie's ambition was just too masculine. In 1911, the academy rejected her—by a single vote. She would never have anything to do with it or its publications again.

Meanwhile, Langevin's wife began making death threats against Marie. In a position to know, Langevin warned Marie to take them seriously; some of her friends were concerned for her safety.

Later in 1911, Marie received two telegrams at almost the same time. Good news and bad news. One telegram informed her that she had just won her second Nobel Prize, this time for Chemistry. It was for essentially the same work as her first Nobel, for Physics, but the Swedish Academy decided that isolating pure radium—which she had done through chemical processes—was "much greater than the discovery of other elements."

Quite a triumph, but the other piece of news was devastating. Those mushy love letters? They'd been leaked to the press. Months earlier, Langevin's wife had hired a detective who managed to steal the letters from Paul's desk at the apartment.

Once the romance hit the newspapers, the scandal was the talk of Paris. Then as now, papers were eager to exploit drama to make money, not only reporting gossip but also fabricating stories. The tabloids throbbed with lurid rumors—was Pierre's death *really* an accident?

All blame fell squarely on Marie, a double standard hard at work. Married men's affairs were often no secret and tolerated by their wives, while a woman's adultery was by law a crime. Marie was a home-wrecker, no longer a "French heroine" but once again a "dirty foreigner" destroying a proper French family. Those who disapproved of a successful woman in a powerful position—one now without a husband to make her more conventionally "acceptable"—railed against her. Some Sorbonne professors demanded that she get out of France. Anti-Semitic writers claimed that she was Jewish.

To some, her behavior was somehow treasonous, a symbol of France's decline. With rivalries among European countries escalating in the pre–World War I years, national pride was a serious issue. The scandal played into France's insecurities that foreign countries were overtaking it.

One newspaper editor published such trashy articles that Langevin challenged him to a duel. Armed with loaded pistols, they met in a park. But at the critical moment, neither could bring himself to fire.

All was silence except for the murmuring of pigeons. Langevin said later, "I am not an assassin," while the editor claimed having last-minute "scruples about depriving French science of a precious brain."

The furor was excruciating for someone so private she dreaded publicity even when it was flattering. Einstein urged Marie to "simply stop reading that drivel," though behind her back he told a friend, "She is not attractive enough to become dangerous for anyone."

Marie tried to fight back. She issued one statement after another, never exactly denying the affair, but objecting to the invasion of her private life: "There is nothing in my acts which obliges me to feel diminished," she insisted. She threatened to sue newspapers, promising to demand "considerable sums which will be used in the interest of science."

But when her house became a tourist attraction, with disapproving Parisians throwing stones at her windows, she finally took her children and left town. Her life in science had to stop for the time being. She grieved at being forced to interrupt her current project in the lab, working with a Dutch physicist to study radiation from radium at very low temperatures.

Marie was crushed. She continued to stand by

Langevin and remain cordial—one friend noted that she was "capable of walking through fire for those she loves"—but it was absolutely unthinkable that they keep seeing each other.

Worst of all, the Nobel Committee tactlessly wrote to ask her to please *not* come to Sweden to accept her prize. In fact, the committee members implied they wouldn't have bestowed it had they known about the love letters. She stood up for herself, indignantly firing a letter back: "I believe there is no connection between my scientific work and the facts of my private life." And off she went to Stockholm to pick up her prize, taking Bronia and Irène for company.

Her dignified speech was not shy about claiming full credit for her accomplishments. Radioactivity "is an infant that I saw being born, and I have contributed to raising it with all my strength. The child has grown; it has become beautiful." She talked about "the chemistry of the imponderable," that scientists were no longer working just with materials they could observe with the naked eye.

But once back in Paris, she was rushed to the hospital, suffering from a kidney ailment as well as the most severe depression of her life. Her weight dropped from 123 to 103 pounds. She had to leave her daughters in the care of family members and governesses. Fearing she was on her deathbed, she wrote seven pages of instructions for the distribution of all the radium in her possession.

She was not to see Ève and Irène for almost a year. For a while, Marie recuperated at the home of an old friend in England. Hertha Ayrton was a scientist (studying, among other things, sand ripples), a nurse, and a militant supporter of women's right to vote. Ayrton had nursed back to health other suffragettes who had carried out hunger strikes in prison; now she applied her ministrations to Marie.

Marie did return home. However, for almost two years, illness hindered her career. She had managed to attend the first Solvay Conference in 1911, sponsored by Ernest Solvay, a wealthy Belgian chemist. He gathered the top twenty-one physicists around the world to discuss the new concepts of Einstein and the German physicist Max Planck. Marie contributed to the lively discussion but made no presentations and left early.

The following year, she was too sick to attend the Solvay Conference. Its ongoing project was to finalize a standard measurement for the amount of radioactivity found in anything. A "standard" sample of radium was needed. From her sickbed, Marie made it known that she would help the project but only on her own terms. For instance, she wanted the standard piece of radium to be kept at *her* lab. She had discovered the element, after all.

Rutherford was brought in to mediate, and although he referred to her as "a rather difficult person to deal with," he managed to bring her around. Although still harboring a protective, almost motherly attitude toward radium, she worked to establish the standard, then in 1913 dutifully handed over the necessary amount of radium in person to the committee. Kept in a safe at the Office of Weights and Measures in Sèvres, the radium was to be made available to five continents. The committee agreed to call the standard unit of measurement a "curie"—the name by which it is known to this day.

Paul Langevin quietly went back to his wife. Marie closed herself to the possibility of love and concentrated on getting the Radium Institute off the ground.

She was having great difficulty regaining her full health, when a new crisis made all her previous troubles seem small.

CHAPTER NINE

War Heroine

*O*N JULY OF 1914, war broke out, first between Austria-Hungary and Serbia, then widening across Europe, eventually pulling in some twenty-five countries, including the United States. As the deadliest confrontation in history so far, the Great War interrupted Marie's work. Science that wasn't war-related was put on hold.

"Senseless" was Marie's word for war: "It is hard to think that after so many centuries of development, the human race still doesn't know how to resolve difficulties in any way except by violence." But while condemning the notion of war, she was determined to help France however she could, possibly also hoping to repair her tarnished reputation. First she offered to donate her prize medals when France asked citizens to donate their gold and silver (the offer was refused).

Then she carried out a daring mission at great personal risk. In September of 1914, after Germany dropped three bombs on Paris, the French president moved the government headquarters outside of Paris to Bordeaux. He worried that if Paris was captured, the valuable radium would fall into German hands and be used somehow against France. He assigned Marie to transport all the radium in France to Bordeaux.

With each tube encased in lead, it was such a heavy suitcase that people wonder to this day how she carried it. A young soldier on the train shared a sandwich with her and asked if she was Marie Curie. She gave her usual denial, in part from her abhorrence of publicity but also for fear that other passengers might think she was a coward fleeing Paris.

From the start, the death tolls were staggering—obscenely so. By November 1914, there would be 310,000 dead, and 300,000 wounded soldiers in France. Scientific "progress" had created new weapons; the Germans were concocting deadly gases like mustard and chlorine, never used before in warfare. Marie's friend and nurse Hertha Ayrton invented a fan to blow the gases out of trenches, and Marie, too, was galvanized to do something healing for French soldiers. "We must act, *act*," she said, putting her research aside—and inspiring her daughter Irène, now seventeen, to join forces with her.

She learned that doctors on the battlefield had no X-ray equipment or technicians available to show where wounded soldiers had been hit by bullets and shrapnel. At the frontlines, wounded men were simply put in ambulances, "in a mixture of mud and blood," as she described it, often dying on the way to a hospital. She knew X-rays could help save lives, so she invented a portable X-ray machine that could be transported to battlefields where it could immediately spot the location of a bullet, for example, inside a soldier's body. Then she struggled for funding for an ambulance. Women drivers were still quite rare, but she got her license so she could drive to the front herself. But still she was not satisfied: she wanted to do more.

So next she commandeered all unused X-ray and automotive equipment in Paris. She assembled a fleet of cars (even limousines), installing X-ray machines inside that could be hooked up to a car battery if electricity wasn't available. Keeping careful notebooks about everything, she trained 150 women technicians to go to the war front.

By 1916, she was Director of the Red Cross Radiology Service, overseeing mobile X-ray units, which became known as "little curies." She was unstoppable, unflappable, ingenious. Again proving herself to be her mother's daughter, she even mastered the basics of car repair so she could take care of breakdowns on the field herself.

She was more than ably assisted by Irène, who was unusually intrepid for her age. Irène taught radiology classes to the military doctors and nurses, went to battle sites and performed X-rays herself, and drew diagrams showing exactly where to operate, sometimes arguing with doctors suspicious of her expertise. She described one doctor as "the enemy of the most elementary notions of geometry" while he was probing a patient's wound. Neither Irène nor Marie bothered to take any precautions against excessive exposure to X-rays, the dangers of which were little known at the time.

Marie's contributions to the war didn't end with

her fleet of X-ray units. In 1917, she also assisted Paul Langevin in inventing an early form of sonar that could capture ultrasonic vibrations—from deadly German submarines, for example.

Paint containing her discovery, radium, also proved useful to the military. Soldiers in the trenches were wearing a new type of watch, one that strapped onto their wrists. The soldiers needed to be able to tell time in the dark. Radium-based paint was used to make luminous numbers on the watch faces, as well as to highlight the dials of instruments on ships, planes, and tanks.

After four long years, World War I ended in November 1918. The joint forces of France, Italy, Great Britain, and the United States finally defeated Germany and its allies.

On the day victory was announced, Marie was in her lab. It was a day for celebration, and she rushed out to buy red, white, and blue material. With help, she sewed giant French flags to hang from the windows. She rejoiced further when news broke that for the first time in 123 years, Poland was liberated from foreign rule. An independent nation once again. Ignacy Jan Paderewski, the famous pianist and an old friend from her early Paris days, became free Poland's first prime minister.

In France, the war had left one out of every six young men in the army dead—1,333,000. The figure would have been even higher had not more than a million X-ray procedures been performed on wounded soldiers. A medical technique in limited use before 1914 became standard practice by war's end. American military doctors, before leaving for home, got training from Marie in X-ray procedures. After this, no surgeon would think of removing a bullet without precise knowledge of its location. This was due in large part to Marie Curie.

Now that it was peacetime, she did what she always did—she got back to work. The first order of business was writing *Radiology in War*. The beneficial use of X-rays was proof that pure science improved lives, although "only through peaceful means can we achieve an ideal society."

Madame Curie was now at the high point of her fame. And as Einstein pointed out, "Marie Curie is, of all celebrated beings, the only one whom fame has not corrupted." By now, she'd learned that fame could be useful, after all—a tool for fulfilling her humanitarian wish to "ease human suffering."

The world "needs dreamers," she said, and society should support them so that their lives "could be freely devoted to the service of scientific research." She hoped to carry her words into action through the Radium Institute, her ultimate and long-postponed dream. After the war, in 1918, the buildings—two pavilions, with a rose garden in between—were opened at last.

CHAPTER TEN

Madame Curie

ARIE CURIE'S RADIUM Institute became one of the great research centers of the world. Its purpose was to study the chemistry of radioactive substances and to search for their medical applications. Through her institute Marie was providing shoulders on which the next generation of researchers could stand.

She ran the lab, keeping forty carefully selected researchers on staff, the best and brightest she could find (though talented women and Poles had a slight edge). Quietly but efficiently, researchers made breakthroughs.

A medical doctor, Claudius Regaud, headed the side of the Radium Institute devoted to medical advances, primarily in the treatment of cancer. Marie followed the work with great interest but didn't contribute directly. Her discovery, radium, was now used in radium therapy, called curietherapy. Doctors exposed patients to tiny amounts of radiation in the attempt to kill their tumors and cure them. The radium might be implanted under the patient's skin, injected, or even swallowed! Early radiation sessions were very long, with patients given books to read and—unfortunately—cigarettes to smoke while waiting.

Between 1919 and 1934, under Marie's serene guidance, the Institute published nearly five hundred books and papers, while its doctors treated over eight thousand patients. It was a small city, where she kept herself aware of every detail, multitasking her days away for a worthy cause. Marie, according to Regaud, "under a cold exterior and the utmost reserve . . . concealed in reality an abundance of delicate and generous feelings."

Among her top priorities was the need to stockpile radium for use at the Institute as well as for scientists all over the world. Unfortunately, radium had become the most expensive substance in the world, approximately $3 million for a single ounce. As much as she hated wasting time with public relations, she did it. Publicity helped get money, and she played a part in exaggerating the highs and lows of her own career—the legend of Marie the martyr—in order to raise precious funds.

Americans were among her most devoted fans, entranced by the story of Marie. (Except for one chemist at Yale, who once called her "a plain darn fool . . . pathetic," and later stated, "I feel sorry for the poor old girl.") Newspapers had headlines like "Curie Cures Cancer!" and "The Greatest Woman in the World." So to the United States Marie set sail, in 1921, with her two daughters. She did long to see the Grand Canyon and Niagara Falls, but the main purpose of the trip was fund-raising. She gave numer-ous college lectures, shook so many hands she had to wear a sling on her right arm, and collected honorary doctorates, medals, and membership in academies. The president of Harvard compared her to Isaac Newton, while *The New York Times* called her "a motherly-looking scientist in a plain black frock." (Her best dress was still the same one she had worn to both Nobel ceremonies.)

The grand finale was an invitation to the White House, where President Warren G. Harding presented her with a gram of radium, almost doubling what she had. This gram was made possible by a $100,000 gift from the American Association of University Women. To women in America—who'd won the right to vote only a year earlier in 1920—she was a heroine, a role model. She was proof that women, even women with families, could become groundbreaking scientists.

Madame Curie's radium stash was unrivaled until the appearance, after 1930, of accelerators that could produce radium in large quantities. Her hoard of radium made a decisive contribution to experiments undertaken for years afterward, especially those performed by Irène Curie, who was maturing into the superstar researcher at the Institute.

What remained was the still vexing question of how much exposure to radiation was too much. Marie was so determined that radium would benefit humanity that she tended to be blind to evidence that it might also harm. Usually she (as well as other scientists) maintained a certain state of denial about radiation sickness. But her own husband, Pierre, was possibly the first person to suffer from its effects. So sometimes she did admit its existence, but minimized its risks, viewing it as an annoyance, a hangnail instead of a death sentence. And so what if you had to put yourself in danger pursuing the noble cause of discovery? In her eyes, those who worried didn't have a serious commitment to science.

And no one else paid much attention to the question until 1925, when a young factory worker in New Jersey sued her employer after nine of her coworkers had died. They were dubbed "The Radium Girls."

The women painted luminous numbers with radium-based paint on the dials of the newly popular wristwatches. To get the finest point on their brushes, the women were instructed to lick them. As a result, they were ingesting tiny amounts of radium. Some weren't affected, and some were—their teeth began to fall out, their jawbones deteriorated, the women weakened and died a painful death. At least fifteen women died at one factory before doctors finally began to realize that even a small amount of radium was highly poisonous.

Today it's a known fact that exposure to radiation poisons the body and actually causes cancer. It interferes with cell division, lodges in the bones, damages tissue, and creates abnormalities. Anemia and leukemia are frequently the results.

As for Marie, she recommended feeding raw liver to anyone who fell ill. In her mind, the fact that she was still alive—after such prolonged contact with radium—meant other people's lack of exercise and fresh air was the cause of their sickness. But she wasn't the picture of health, and she knew it. For years she'd had numbness in her fingers and obsessively rubbed them with her thumb to restore sensation. Her hearing was going, there was a constant humming in her ears, she was nearly blind from cataracts, and she suffered from fatigue and other ailments she blamed on overwork. She rarely went to doctors, none of whom made the connection between her symptoms and radium. In any case, no treatment would have been available. After several suspiciously premature deaths at the Institute, she installed stricter safety rules—people had to wear lead shields and could not handle radium with bare hands—but didn't follow them herself. Always, her messages about radium's safety were mixed.

Meanwhile, after her courageous war work and the achievements of her Institute, she became a heroine in France again. Even an icon. At a celebration in her honor at the Paris Opéra, all the notables in France thanked her for her contributions to science. The actress Sarah Bernhardt read "Ode to Madame Curie," which called her a goddess. And in science circles, the reputation of her Institute was rising ever higher.

Another thrilling achievement was the 1932 opening of a second Radium Institute, in Warsaw. Her own sister Bronia became its director.

Every morning, a chauffeur drove Marie in a Ford (a gift from Henry Ford himself) to work. She continued to write books, swim, take snowshoe walks in the Alps to get the best views of sunsets. She was, at last, financially secure, and bought several vacation homes. Yet still, her most cherished time was working with Irène long hours into the night.

So many more things she wanted to accomplish. "It is sad that one can't be doubled," she wrote toward the end of her life.

CHAPTER ELEVEN

Genius Genes

*O*N HER OWN daughter, Marie did produce a sort of double.

One day when Irène was a little girl, she electrified other children with an exact biological description of how babies were made. By the time she reached her teens, she was allowed to teach math and physics to her classmates.

Already in Marie's own lifetime, she was inspiring young women to think science. Irène was just one of the many who idolized Marie.

When Irène was ten, Marie denied she was pushing her child into science: "She will be whatever she

wants to be. All I ask of her right now is that she be healthy." But Irène was clearly another brainiac, and Marie *was* a bit pushy. Once, when her daughter couldn't come up with the correct answer to a problem, she threw Irène's algebra notebook out the window into the garden two stories down. As her own father had done so many years before, Marie mailed Irène advanced math challenges to work on when they were apart. As her own mother had hinted that the better her children did at school, the more she loved them, Marie was at her fondest when Irène excelled.

As she grew up, Irène seemed nearly as driven as her mother. At the same time as she was tending to soldiers on the warfront, she managed to gradu-ate from the Sorbonne *with honors* in math, physics, and chemistry. At the Institute, Irène was known as the Princess and was clearly being groomed as her mother's successor.

Many American women were also inspired by Marie to pursue careers in science. When she visited the United States in 1921, only 41 women were work-ing on doctorates in science. But by 1932 it was 138, with chemistry a favorite specialty.

Closer to home was the chemist Marguerite Perey, who started out at the Radium Institute as a test-tube washer. She went on to discover the radioactive element francium in 1939, and eventually became the first woman elected to the French Academy of Sciences in 1962, fifty-one years after Marie's humili-ating rejection.

Young boys found Marie inspirational as well. In France, one of them was Frédéric Joliot. He kept a photo of the Curies taped to his bedroom wall. As a promising young man he studied under Paul Langevin, who sent him over to Marie to be an assistant at the Institute. (Langevin also sent over a woman student he had had a child with, asking Marie to find her a job, which she did.)

Irène Curie married Frédéric in 1926. They took the joint name Joliot-Curie and began to work together in fine Marie-Pierre fashion. Marie disapproved of her son-in-law at first and worried he would take control of the Institute and its radium. But she soon came to realize what a "ball of fire" Frédéric Joliot was. In a complete turnabout, she urged him to get his advanced degrees and helped him develop as a scientist. The Curies were growing into a sort of royal dynasty.

At first the golden couple hit some frustrating roadblocks in their work. Their experiments pointed the way for others to make important discoveries, ones that filled in "missing pieces" in the anatomy of the atom.

Performing the same experiments as the Joliot-Curies, one of Rutherford's assistants, James Chadwick, discovered the neutron. And in California in 1932, Carl David Anderson discovered what he called a positron, or positive electron. The Joliot-Curies had produced the same results as Chadwick but come to different conclusions. Frédéric wrote, "It is annoying to be overtaken by other laboratories which immediately take up one's experiments."

Still, Marie must have drawn considerable satisfaction at the seventh Solvay Conference of distinguished physicists in 1933, this one dedicated to nuclear physics. No longer was she the only woman in attendance. Besides Irène, there was also a German physicist, Lise Meitner.

And Marie also lived to see the stunning success in creating "artificial" radioactivity that put the Joliot-Curies on the map.

When they showed a frail Marie chemical proof of what they'd done, using her cherished element polonium in experiments, Frédéric noted "the expression of intense joy" on Marie's face. "This was doubtless the last great satisfaction of her life." Because of her daughter and son-in-law, her work would continue on.

On her last day at work, Marie grew frustrated with an experiment not going well and left the lab early with fever and chills, mentioning to a gardener on her way out that the roses needed pruning. For two months, she lay sick in bed, finally succumbing on July 4, 1934. Her last words were "I want to be left in peace." She was sixty-seven years old. Beyond a doubt, the cause of death was her decades-long exposure to radiation, even though her attitude remained mixed to the end: "Perhaps radium has something to do with [my] troubles, but it cannot be affirmed with certainty."

After her funeral, she was buried next to Pierre, with her sister Bronia arriving to drop a handful of Polish soil into the grave.

Sadly, Marie missed her daughter's day of greatest triumph. It came the following year. Irène Joliot-Curie became the second woman in history to win the Nobel Prize for chemistry. She and Frédéric (co-winner) both gave acceptance speeches, predicting "explosive" transmutations to come.

Indeed, their work speeded up the development of nuclear physics. The ability to create radioactivity artificially, in a lab, was a major step toward unlocking the secrets of an atom's energy. Scientists were that much closer to figuring out how to release nuclear power and harness it. Both Irène and Frédéric hoped nuclear power would be used for peaceful purposes, like supplying energy to France to undercut the need for imported oil.

But World War II intervened, and the course of nuclear physics headed straight in the direction that Marie Curie and the Joliot-Curies feared most.

Building on Marie's work and the work of the Joliot-Curies, scientists in the United States made the first atomic bomb.

In August of 1945, determined to end the long war, the United States dropped atomic bombs on two Japanese cities, first Hiroshima and then Nagasaki. Radiation's full fury was unleashed, with over 100,000 people in Hiroshima instantly vaporized. Japan surrendered, and World War II was over.

Yes, the war ended. But suddenly warfare had taken on new dimensions. Now there were weapons capable of destruction on a scale never before seen. Besides those who were killed, hundreds of thousands more Japanese people suffered radiation sickness—burned and singed, their hair falling out, with persistent vomiting, and then long-term effects like leukemia and other cancers, their babies born with birth defects for years afterward.

Appalled, Irène said that she was glad Marie Curie, dead for eleven years, was no longer alive to bear witness. The dropping of atom bombs was a shocking event, to many the most shocking of the century. More than sixty years later, controversy still lingers over the decision.

In 1950, Frédéric Joliot-Curie was dismissed from the French Atomic Energy Commission for refusing to work on an atomic bomb. Irène, too, was an advocate for world peace and a member of the Nuclear Disarmament Peace Council. More politically active than her mother, she also worked for women's rights, helping to finally get the vote for French women in 1945.

In 1956, Irène died at age fifty-nine of leukemia brought on by—what else?—exposure to radium. Almost too ill himself to visit his wife's deathbed, Frédéric died two years later from the same illness.

Years later, proving how small the world of French science was, Marie's granddaughter Hélène married the grandson of Paul Langevin (Marie's lover), extending the dynasty. Hélène became a leading particle physicist in the 1950s, studying the polarization of electrons emitted through decay. By 1957, she was director of research at the Institute of Nuclear Physics, a 580-person lab.

And what about Ève, Marie's younger daughter?

Her gift was for music, which didn't impress Marie as much as Irène's accomplishments in science. Ève's rela-tionship with Marie was not as smooth. "You torture your brows, you daub at your lips," her mother would scold. "I like you when you're not so tricked up. . . . You'll never make me believe women were meant to walk on stilts. . . . Miles and miles of naked back! You run the risk of pleurisy."

But the fashion-conscious Ève grew up to become healthy, independent, idealistic, a fighter for the French Resistance against the Nazis, and a war correspondent whose knowledge of German was helpful to the Allies. In 1937, she lovingly wrote and published a biography of her mother. One of the best-selling biographies of all time, it had the effect of making Marie Curie even more of an inspiration to young girls. Ève attained her own Nobel fame by working with her husband Henri Labouisse. He was director of UNICEF, the United Nations program devoted to the welfare of children, when it was awarded the Nobel Peace Prize in 1965. Never having worked directly with radium, Ève was not exposed to its deadly rays. She is still alive at 102.

Today we know for certain that Marie, Pierre, Irène, and Frédéric all suffered from radiation sickness.

One of the great mysteries in science is why Marie didn't die earlier—perhaps she really was unusually strong physically, or just inhumanly stubborn psychologically. Everything she touched, even her notebooks, remained so contaminated with radiation that until recently people had to sign a medical release before looking at her original papers.

But would Marie have changed anything? Probably not. "Life is not easy for any of us," she once wrote. "But what of that? We must have perseverance and above all confidence in ourselves. We must believe we are gifted for something, and that this thing, at whatever cost, must be attained."

In other words, great science requires great sacrifice. She certainly lived by her own words.

CHAPTER TWELVE

How She Changed the World

*A*S MUCH AS she pooh-poohed the role of personality in science, Marie Curie's celebrity carried a lot of weight. Although not single-handedly, she did pave the way to a new era in medicine, plus she laid the groundwork for seismic developments in physics and chemistry. Because of her, scientists had new ways of thinking about matter and energy.

The discovery of radium opened the new field of radioactivity. In the years since, radium has been put to use in a boggling number of ways. Most important, radium offered an effective means to treat cancer. By the mid-1950s, doctors began refining radiation therapy by replacing radium with another element, cobalt—much safer, cheaper, and more effective. Today radiation therapy is just one weapon in an arsenal of cancer treatments. Meanwhile, scientists continue to look for a cure for the disease.

From the study of radioactivity came radiocarbon-dating techniques. Since we know the half-lives of various forms of the element carbon, we can use them to ascertain the ages of carbon-containing fossils, rocks, and other archeological finds. From such work have come measurements indicating that our Earth is four billion years old.

Various industries use radioactivity, with strict safety precautions. The food industry, for example, uses it to kill organisms that cause disease and spoil food. Companies that manufacture film, lenses, and other items use radioactivity to remove static-causing dust.

Perhaps most important of all, Marie's work led to a redefinition of the atom, which, since ancient times, was considered unchangeable and indivisible. Quite the opposite—it turned out that the atom is like a universe, containing whole worlds inside it.

Nuclear power—despite its potential dangers—still offers a source of plentiful energy less damaging to the environment than energy from fossil fuels. Today, thanks in part to Marie's son-in-law Frédéric, France's nuclear power plants generate 80 percent of the country's energy.

The United States uses nuclear power to provide about 20 percent of the electricity it uses. Such a policy remains hotly debated. Nuclear accidents can and do occur, the worst occurring in the Ukraine in 1986. At the Chernobyl Nuclear Power Plant, an accidental explosion released 100 million curies of radioactive material, killing dozens immediately. Three hundred thousand people had to be evacuated. Over six million people across Russia and Europe were exposed to contamination. Some scientists predict that premature death rates from cancer and other diseases will be higher than normal among the exposed, though estimates vary widely.

Harnessing nuclear energy can be the hope of the world—or it can be the agent of its destruction. After the bombing of Hiroshima and Nagasaki, Albert Einstein mourned the events and considered himself as well as other scientists obligated to make sure atomic weapons were never used again.

Since 1945, nuclear weapons have not been used. But the threat hovers. The United States is no lon- ger the only country with the technology to make an atom bomb. More and more countries have atomic bombs of their own, and we pay close attention to which ones are stashing uranium, the first building block of a bomb.

For better or worse, Marie helped to create the modern world.

She also helped create the modern woman, not solely those women who wanted to pursue a career in science but, of course, most especially them. In 1943, a movie about her (*Madame Curie*, starring the glamor- ous Greer Garson) inspired countless girls who could feel less oddball for liking science. "I believe that men's and women's scientific aptitudes are exactly the same," Irène once told a reporter—not something you heard very often before Marie's time.

The Curie-Joliot-Langevin dynasty also represented a new era when scientists worked together, as teams in large labs, often without a solo superstar. It is impos- sible to imagine the brilliant but reclusive Isaac New- ton, who hoarded his discoveries like treasure, working at an institute like the one the Curies founded. The papers of Marie's granddaughter Hélène, for example, give credit to as many as twenty scientists' contributions.

Knowing she was an icon, Marie tried to reassure women that they didn't *have* to be as obsessed as she was: "It isn't necessary to lead such an anti-natural existence as mine. I have given a great deal of time to science because I wanted to, because I loved research. . . . What I want for women and young girls is a simple family life and some work that will interest them." She advocated a more balanced life than her own.

And yet it was that very lack of balance that made her Marie Curie. Against all the obstacles she faced, how did she accomplish so much? She was lucky enough to have a support system within her own family: a well-educated mother, a father who never discouraged her, relatives who broadened her horizons. Bronia provided a superb role model, Pierre thought she was a genius, and her daughters recognized her for the heroine she was. From her childhood in Poland, under the thumb of Russian rule, she learned how to resist authority and fight for what she wanted. Most of all, she was fueled by a drive to succeed, capable of burying herself in her work to the exclusion of all else.

Since Marie Curie, ten more women have won Nobel Prizes in science, and the number of women scientists has been steadily climbing. Today in the United States, of the students earning advanced science degrees, four out of ten are women.

Schools and streets, stamps and coins have been named for Marie. Every place she ever lived has a plaque honoring her. Her beloved Institute continues to thrive in Paris, coordinating the work of 1,700 people in physics, chemistry, biology, and medicine, with the prevention, diagnosis, and treatment of cancer as its objective. Every year, some 75,000 people seek help there, drawn by its philosophy: "Marie Curie's rigorous moral and intellectual approach, as well as her humility and modesty have forged our values and the 'Curie' approach."

Marie even has her own element. In 1944, scientists at University of California, Berkeley, discovered another new one, number 96, which they named "curium" in her and Pierre's honor. Today we recognize some 120 elements, 92 in nature and the others created artificially in labs.

Not until 1938, four years after Marie's death, were radioactive materials banned from products for consumers. Organizations now exist to monitor radiation safety nationally and internationally. But the question of how much radiation is too much is still a subject of debate among scientists.

In 1995, Marie's ashes, along with Pierre's, were transferred from the cemetery in Sceaux to the Panthéon. At this monument for heroes in Paris, the inscription reads, "To Great Men from a Grateful Country." As with so many other firsts in her life, she was the first woman to be buried at the Panthéon because of her own achievements. Thousands gathered along the streets to watch, while the president of France spoke about "the first lady of our honored history . . . who decided to impose her abilities in a society where abilities, intellectual exploration, and public responsibility were reserved for men."

With perverse interest, scientists measured the radiation coming from her casket. Oddly enough, they found it to be less than expected, given her exposure to so many radioactive substances.

Marie wouldn't have considered herself a martyr to science. In fact, she said, "I am among those who think that science has a great beauty. A scientist in his laboratory is not only a technician, he is also a child placed before natural phenomena, which impress him like a fairy tale."

Science was beautiful and adventurous, a game she enjoyed, and one she played to win.

BIBLIOGRAPHY

(* books especially for young readers)

Brian, Denis. *The Curies: A Biography of the Most Controversial Family in Science.* Hoboken, N.J.: John Wiley & Sons, 2005.

* Cooney, Miriam P., ed. *Celebrating Women in Mathematics and Science.* Reston, Va.: National Council of Teachers of Mathematics, 1996.

Curie, Eve. *Madame Curie: A Biography,* with a new introduction by Natalie Angier. New York: Da Capo Press, 2001.

* Dendy, Leslie, and Mel Boring. *Guinea Pig Scientists: Bold Self-Experimenters in Science and Medicine.* New York: Holt, 2005.

Goldsmith, Barbara. *Obsessive Genius: The Inner World of Marie Curie.* New York: W. W. Norton, 2005.

* McClafferty, Carla Killough. *Something Out of Nothing: Marie Curie and Radium.* New York: Farrar, Straus and Giroux, 2006.

* Pasachoff, Naomi. *Marie Curie and the Science of Radioactivity.* New York: Oxford University Press, 1996.

Pflaum, Rosalynd. *Grand Obsession: Madame Curie and Her World.* New York: Doubleday, 1989.

* Pflaum, Rosalynd. *Marie Curie and Her Daughter Irène.* Minneapolis: Lerner, 1993.

Preston, Diana. *Before the Fallout: From Marie Curie to Hiroshima.* New York: Berkley Books, 2005.

Quinn, Susan. *Marie Curie: A Life.* New York: Da Capo Press, 1995.

* **Steele, Philip.** *Marie Curie: The Woman Who Changed the Course of Science.* Washington, D.C.: National Geographic Children's Books, 2006.

* **Strathern, Paul.** *Curie and Radioactivity: The Big Idea.* London: Arrow Books, 1998.

WEB SITES

(Verified June 2007)

"How Nuclear Radiation Works": http://science.howstuffworks.com/nuclear.htm

Institut Curie, Paris: http://www.curie.fr/index.cfm/lang/_gb.htm (includes the Curie Museum)

"Madame Curie," National Atomic Museum: http://www.atomicmuseum.com/tour/curie.cfm

"Marie Curie: Biography," http://nobelprize.org/physics/laureates/1903/marie-curie-bio.html

"Marie Curie: A Nobel Prize Pioneer at the Panthéon": http://www.diplomatie.gouv.fr/label_france/ENGLISH/SCIENCES/CURIE/marie.html

"Marie Curie, Radioactivity, and the Emerging New Physics: The Extraordinary Career of a Woman Scientist," Yale School of Medicine: http://info.med.yale.edu/library/exhibits/curie/welcome.html

"Marie Curie and the Science of Radioactivity," American Institute of Physics: http://www.aip.org/history/curie

"Marie and Pierre Curie and the Discovery of Polonium and Radium," Nobel Prize Official Site: http://nobelprize.org/physics/articles/curie/index.html

Museum of Maria Sklodowska-Curie, Warsaw: http://www.ptchem.lodz.pl/en/museum.html

The Periodic Table of Elements, Jefferson Lab: http://education.jlab.org/itselemental/

INDEX

alchemy, 11

alpha rays, 69–70, 79

American Association of University Women, 111

Anderson, Carl David, 118

anti-Semitism, 95

atom

    believed to be the smallest particle of matter, 9, 35–36, 126

    structure of, 89, 118

    subatomic particles, discovery of, 9–10, 57–58, 89

atomic physics, 118–19

    see also nuclear physics

atomic weapons, 10, 120–22, 127–28

Ayrton, Hertha, 98, 103

Becquerel, Henri, 13, 44–46, 55, 74, 77

Bernhardt, Sarah, 31, 114

beta rays, 69, 79

Boyle, Robert, 11

cancer

    radiation exposure as cause of, 112–13, 122, 127

    radiation (radium) therapy for, 9, 65–66, 80, 109, 125–26, 130

Cassatt, Mary, 31

Chadwick, James, 118–19

chemistry, 46

    early history of, 11–12

    Mendeleyev's periodic table of elements, 12, 13, 34–35, 51, 68–69, 88, 130

Chernobyl Nuclear Power Plant, 127

cobalt, 126

Comte, Auguste, 24, 25

curie (unit of measurement), 98–99

Curie, Ève, *see* Labouisse, Ève Curie (Marie's daughter)

Curie, Irène, *see* Joliot-Curie, Irène (Marie's daughter)

Curie, Jacques, 40

Curie, Marie (née Sklowdowska), 10–11

    ambition, 57, 62, 93, 130

    biography written by daughter Ève, 123

    burial at the Panthéon, 131

    childhood of, 15–23, 129

    collaboration with Pierre, 13, 53–57, 60–66, 70–71, 72–73

    dangers of radiation exposure and, 13–14, 64–65, 111–13, 120, 123–24

    death of, 119–20, 124

    depression and, 19–20, 29, 87, 97

    education of, 17–19, 20–22, 24, 25, 27–28, 29, 32–37, 42–43, 72

    fame of, 75–77, 110, 113–14, 130

    finances of, 70–71, 75, 77–78, 114

    fund-raising by, 110–11

    as governess, 27, 28–29

    hard work and, 10–11, 61–62, 68, 69, 81–82

    health of, 13–14, 68, 75, 97–98, 113, 120, 123

    legacy of, 125–32

    love affairs of, 27, 28, 30, 92–97

    marriage of, 42

    miscarriage, 75

    as mother, 48, 62, 77, 86, 90–91, 96, 98, 115–17

    Nobel prizes, 8, 74–75, 77, 82, 97

notebooks, 53, 62, 87–88, 104, 124
patience and persistence of,
  10–11, 61–62, 68, 124
personality of, 10, 21, 109
Pierre's death and, 84–87
Polish name, 15
supernatural and, 71–72
as teacher and lecturer, 71, 90, 91
Curie, Pierre (husband), 61–62, 120
burial at the Panthéon, 131
career as scientist, 39, 40, 41, 49
collaboration with Marie, 13,
  53–57, 60–66, 70–71, 72–73
courtship of Marie, 37–42
dangers of radiation exposure and,
  13–14, 64–65
death of, 84–87, 95
described, 39–41
education of, 40, 41
fame and, 75–77, 81
father of, 48–49, 86–87, 91
finances of, 70–71, 75, 77–78
health of, 13–14, 68, 75, 83, 111, 123
marriage of, 42
Nobel prizes, 8, 74–75, 77, 82
supernatural and, 71–72
support for Marie's research and
  studies, 42–43, 49–50, 129
as teacher at the Sorbonne, 71,
  78, 91
curium, discovery and naming of, 130

Darwin, Charles, 80
Debierne, André-Louis, 66
Demarcay, Eugène, 54
Dickens, Charles, 21
Duclaux, Emile, 34

Einstein, Albert, 81, 89, 92, 96, 98, 106,
  127–28
electrometer, 40, 50

electrons, 58, 89, 93, 122
Elementary Treatise on Chemistry
  (Lavoisier), 12
elements, 130
defined, 11, 12
first table of, 12
Mendeleyev's periodic table, 12,
  13, 34–35, 51, 68–69, 88, 130
see also specific elements
energy, laws of, 67

"Flying University," 24
Ford, Henry, 67, 114
fractional crystallization, 61
French Academy of Sciences, 46, 51,
  55, 56
Pierre Curie elected to, 78
Marie Curie's rejection by, 93–94,
  117
first woman elected to, 117
as male institution, 78
French Atomic Energy Commission,
  122
French Resistance, 123
Freud, Sigmund, 67, 86

gallium, discovery of, 35
Garson, Greer, 128
germanium, discovery of, 35

half-life of unstable elements, 80
radiocarbon-dating techniques,
  80, 126
Harding, Warren G., 111
Harvard University, 110
helium, 54
Hiroshima, 121, 127

Institute of Nuclear Physics, 122
International Congress of Physics, 1900,
  67

Interpretation of Dreams, The (Freud), 67

Japan, atomic bombs used against, 121–22
Joliot-Curie, Frédéric, 117–19, 122, 127
    death of, 122, 123
    Nobel Prize, 120
Joliot-Curie, Irène (Marie's daughter), 8, 76, 129
    childhood of, 48–49, 62, 84, 86 87, 90–91, 96, 97, 98, 115–17
    death of, 122, 123
    education of, 91, 116–17
    Nobel Prize, 120
    at Radium Institute, 111, 114, 117, 118–19
    as world peace advocate, 122
    during World War I, 104

Labouisse, Ève Curie (daughter), 122–23, 129
    biography of her mother, 123
    childhood of, 77, 81–82, 84, 86–87, 90–91, 96, 98
    education of, 91
Labouisse, Henri, 123
Langevin, Hélène (granddaughter of Marie Curie), 122, 129
Langevin, Paul, 92–97, 99, 105, 117
Lavoisier, Antoine-Laurent, 12
Lippmann, Gabriel, 34
"little curies," (X-ray machine), 104
Lumière, Auguste and Louis, 43

Madame Curie (1943 film), 128
    magnetic properties of steel, Marie Curie's research on, 36, 41, 46
medical uses of radium, 9, 65–66, 70, 80, 108, 109, 125–26, 130
Meitner, Lise, 119

Mendeleyev, Dmitri, 12, 34–35, 88–89
Model T, 67
Monet, Claude, 31
"Museum of Industry and Agriculture," 29

Nagasaki, 121, 127
neutron, discovery of, 118–19
"New Radioactive Substances and the Rays They Emit, The," 67
Newton, Sir Isaac, 8, 11, 54, 65, 110, 128–29
New York Times, The, 110
Nobel, Alfred, 74
Nobel Prize, recipients of, 123, 130
    Henri Becquerel, 74
    Marie and Pierre Curie, 8, 74–75, 77, 82, 94, 97
    Irène and Frédéric Joliot-Curie, 120
    Gabriel Lippman, 34
    Wilhelm Röntgen, 74
Nuclear Disarmament Peace Council, 122
nuclear physics, 89, 118–19
    atomic weapons and, 120–22
    peaceful applications of, 120
    see also atomic physics
nuclear power, 127
nucleus of the atom, 89

"On a New Radio-Active Substance Contained in Pitchblende," 55
"On Symmetry in Physical Phenomena," 41
Orzeszkowa, Eliza, 25

Paderewski, Jan, 105–6
paint, radium-based, 105, 112
Paris Exposition of 1900, 66–67
Paris School of Industrial Physics and Chemistry, 39

Pasteur, Louis, 13, 88
Pasteur Institute, 88
Perey, Marguerite, 117
pitchblende, 52, 55, 56, 59–60, 67–68
    residue, 60
Planck, Max, 98
Poincaré, Henri, 34
Poland
    liberation of, 105–6
    Russian rule of, 16, 21, 28, 129
polonium, 119
    atomic weight of, 68
    discovery of, 9, 13, 53–55, 59
    half-life of, 81
    researching of, 13
positivism, 24, 25
positron, discovery of the, 118
Principles of Chemistry, The
    (Mendeleyev), 12, 34

quartz crystals, 40, 49

radiation exposure, dangers of, 13–14,
    64–65, 123–24
    determining lethal levels of
        exposure, 66, 111–13, 131
radioactivity, 57, 77, 78, 79, 81, 88–89,
    97, 125
    "artificial," 119, 120
    commercial uses of, 126
    half-life of unstable elements, 80
    the paranormal and, 72
    Treatise on Radioactivity, 88
radiocarbon-dating techniques, 80, 126
Radiology in War (Curie), 106
radium
    atomic weight of, 68
    in consumer products, 78–79, 112,
        131
    cost per ounce, 109–10
    dangers of exposure to, *see*
        radiation exposure, dangers of

discovery of, 9, 11, 13, 56, 59, 68, 125
    isolation of pure, 59–62, 64,
        67–68, 82, 88, 94
    medical uses of, *see* medical uses
        of radium
    military applications of, 105
    patent for producing, 70
    predictions of potential for evil
        from, 82–83
    production in large quantities, 111
    researching of, 13, 65–66, 69, 77
    research leading to discovery of,
        50–56
    safekeeping of, during World
        War I, 102
    standard unit of measurement
        ("curie"), 98–99
    as unstable element, 79
Radium Institute, Paris, 13, 99, 108–14,
    117–18, 130
    accomplishments of, 108–109, 130
    building of, 88
    Irène Curie's accomplishments at,
        111, 114, 117, 118–19
    fund-raising for, 110–11
    opening of, 107
    safety rules at, 113
Radium Institute, Warsaw, 114
radium salt, 68
"Rays Emitted by Uranium and
    Thorium Compounds," 51
Red Cross Radiology Service, 104
Regaud, Claudius, 109
relativity, theory of, 81
Röntgen, Wilhelm, 13, 43–44, 46, 57, 74
Rutherford, Ernest, 69–70, 89, 99
    half-life of unstable elements and,
        80
    transformation theory, 79

Schmidt, G. C., 53
science, 131–32

collaboration by scientists, 128–29
female scientists, Marie Curie
as inspiration for, 117, 123, 128,
130
increased public interest in, 77
male scientists, Marie Curie as
inspiration for, 117–18
scientific method, 25, 68
séances, 71–72
Skeptical Chymist, The (Boyle), 11
Sklodowska, Bronia (Marie's sister),
26–27, 29–32, 52, 57, 97, 120, 129
as director of Warsaw Radium
Institute, 114
Sklodowska, Bronislawa (Marie's
mother), 16–17, 116, 129
death of, 19
Sklodowska, Zosia (Marie's sister), 15,
19
Sklodowski, Wladyslaw (Marie's
father), 16, 20–21, 22, 27–28, 30, 37,
116, 129
death of, 69
Sklodowski family, 15, 17
Society for the Encouragement of
National Industry, 36
Solvay, Ernest, 98
Solvay Conferences, 98, 119
sonar, 105
Sorbonne, University of Paris, 30,
32–37, 40, 90, 117
Marie Curie as professor at, 91
Pierre Curie as teacher at, 71,
78, 91
Marie Curie's doctorate from, 72
spectroscopy, 54

theory of relativity, 81
Thomson, J. J., 57–58, 69, 89
thorium, 51, 53
Toulouse-Lautrec, Henri de, 31
Treatise on Radioactivity (Curie), 88

UNICEF, 123
United States
atomic weapons and, 121–22
Marie Curie's 1921 visit to,
110–11, 117
nuclear power in, 127
women's rights in, 111
University of California, Berkeley, 130
University of Paris, 88
University of Zurich, 89
unstable elements, 79, 81
half-life of, 80
uranium, 45, 46–47, 49, 50, 128
half-life of, 80

watches with radium-based paint, 105,
112
women
cultural limits on opportunities
for, 10, 23–24, 25, 32, 33, 74–75,
78, 82, 91, 93–94, 128–29
firsts for, Marie Curie and, 71,
72, 131
Marie Curie as inspiration to
female scientists, 117
rights of, 25, 111, 122
World War I, 101–5
Marie Curie's contributions
during, 101–2, 103–5
death tolls, 102, 106
new weapons used in, 102–3
World War II
atomic weapons used in, 121–22,
127
French Resistance, 123
Wright Brothers, 67

X-ray equipment, 103–5, 106
portable, Marie Curie's invention
of, 103–5
X-rays, 45
discovery of, 13, 43–44